WORKBOOK

FOR THE

GREENPRINT

BY MARCO BORGES

Plant-Based Diet, Best Body, Better World

BY

DEPENDABLE PUBLISHING

COPYRIGHT

This publication is protected under the US Copyright Act of 1976 and other applicable international, federal, state, and local laws. All rights are reserved, including resale rights. You are not allowed to reproduce, transmit or sell this book in parts or in full without the written permission of the publisher. Printed in the USA. Copyright © 2019, Dependable Publishing.

DISCLAIMER

This book is a WORKBOOK. It is meant to be a companion, not a replacement, to the original book. Please note that this workbook is not authorized, licensed, approved, or endorsed by the author or publisher of the main book. The author of this workbook is wholly responsible for the content of this workbook and is not associated with the original author or publisher of the main book in any way. If you are looking to purchase a copy of the main book, please visit Amazon's website and search for "The Greenprint *by Marco Borges*".

TABLE OF CONTENTS

LAW 1: EAT MORE PLANTS AND EAT LESS OF EVERYTHING ELSE 8

- LESSONS 8
- KNOWLEDGE CHECK 8
- ACTION STEPS 10
- CHECKLIST 15

LAW 2: NOBODY EVER PLANS TO FAIL- PEOPLE JUST FAIL TO PLAN 16

- LESSONS 16
- KNOWEDGE CHECK 16
- ACTION STEPS 18
- CHECKLIST 20

LAW 3: EAT MORE, WEIGH LESS 22

- LESSONS 22
- KNOWLEDGE CHECK 22
- ACTION STEPS 23
- CHECKLIST 25

LAW 4: WATER IS LIFE FUEL 26

- LESSONS 26
- KNOWLEDGE CHECK 26
- ACTION STEPS 27

CHECKLIST 28

LAW 5: PROTECT YOUR HEART 29

LESSONS 29

KNOWLEDGE CHECK 29

ACTION STEPS 30

CHECKLIST 31

LAW 6: TAKE CARE OF YOUR MIND 32

LESSONS 32

KNOWLEDGE CHECK 32

ACTION STEPS 33

CHECKLIST 34

LAW 7: FAST FOR HEALTH AND LONGETIVITY   35

LESSONS 35

KNOWLEDGE CHECK 35

ACTION STEPS 36

CHECKLIST 36

LAW 8: THINK ABOUT THE EARTH BEFORE YOU EAT   37

LESSONS 37

KNOWLEDGE CHECK 37

ACTION STEPS 38

CHECKLIST 39

LAW 9: LOVE FOOD THAT LOVES YOU BACK 40

LESSONS 40

- KNOWLEDGE CHECK 40
- ACTION STEPS 41
- CHECKLIST 42

LAW 10: MOVEMENT BEGETS MOVEMENT 43

- LESSONS 43
- KNOWLEDGE CHECK 43
- ACTION STEPS 44
- CHECKLIST 44

LAW 11: TRASH MUST BE TAKEN OUT 45

- LESSONS 45
- KNOWLEDGE CHECK 45
- ACTION STEPS 46
- CHECKLIST 47

LAW 12: THE WORLD DOESN'T NEED US TO SURVIVE – WE NEED THE WORLD TO SURVIVE 48

- LESSONS 48
- KNOWLEDGE CHECK 48
- ACTION STEPS 50
- CHECKLIST 52

LAW 13: CHANGE STARTS WITH YOU 53

- LESSONS 53
- KNOWLEDGE CHECK 53
- ACTION STEPS 54

CHECKLIST 57

LAW 14: THE BEST STARTING POINT IS TODAY   59

LESSONS 59

KNOWLEDGE TEST 59

ACTION STEPS 60

CHECKLIST 62

LAW 15: PERFECTION CAN BE THE ENEMY OF PROGRESS   63

LESSONS 63

KNOWLEDGE CHECK 63

ACTION STEPS 64

CHECKLIST 66

LAW 16: LISTEN TO YOUR BODY 67

LESSONS 67

KNOWLEDGE CHECK 67

ACTION STEPS 69

CHECKLIST 70

LAW 17: FOCUS ON WHAT YOU CAN EAT, NOT WHAT YOU CAN'T 71

LESSONS 71

KNOWLEDGE CHECK 71

ACTION STEPS 72

CHECKLIST 74

LAW 18: PLANTS HAVE ALL THE POWER WE NEED   76

- LESSONS 76
- KNOWLEDGE CHECK 76
- ACTION STEPS 78
- CHECKLIST 78

LAW 19: A BEHAVIOR THAT IS REWARDED WOULD BE REPEATED 80

- LESSONS 80
- KNOWLEDGE CHECK 80
- ACTION STEPS 81
- CHECKLIST 83

LAW 20: YOU CANNOT GIVE WHAT YOU DO NOT HAVE   84

- LESSONS 84
- KNOWLEDGE CHECK 84
- ACTION STEPS 85
- CHECKLIST 85

LAW 21: BRING MINDFULNESS TO EATING 86

- LESSONS 86
- KNOWLEDGE CHECK 86
- ACTION STEPS 87
- CHECKLIST 87

LAW 22: PRACTICE KAIZEN 88

- LESSONS 88
- KNOWLEDGE CHECK 88

- ACTION STEPS ... 89
- CHECKLIST ... 89

PART 2: LIVING THE GREENPRINT LAWS: THE THREE TRANSITIONAL TIERS ... 90

- CHECKLIST FOR LIVING THE GREEN PRINT LAWS ... 90

TIER 1: THE GRADUAL SHIFT ... 91

- CHECKLIST FOR TIER 1: THE GRADUAL SHIFT ... 91

TIER 2: THE RAMP UP ... 92

- CHECKLIST FOR TIER 2: THE RAMP UP ... 92

TIER 3: THE FULL-ON ... 93

- CHECKLIST FOR TIER 3: THE FULL-ON ... 93

CONCLUSION: BE THE GREENPRINT ... 94

APPENDIX A: CERTIFICATE OF COMMITMENT ... 95

APPENDIX B: THE MASTER CHECKLIST ... 96

This is a master checklist of all the action items and important points in the book. Review this master checklist every day and ensure that your thoughts and activities are in line with its prescriptions. Some items on the list are repeated on purpose. Consider that as an indication of their extra importance and just get to working and living this master checklist. It's pleasantly challenging and it's fun. So, make sure you have a lot of fun while going at it! You can do it! It's a lot of fun! Let's go! ... 96

LAW 1: EAT MORE PLANTS AND EAT LESS OF EVERYTHING ELSE

LESSONS

- Plants are life. Eat more plants, vegetables. Also eat plenty of fruits, including legumes, beans, nuts, seeds, and whole grains.
- A plant-based diet can revitalize your body and your health.
- A 100% plant-based diet is the only diet that is known to be effective for preventing, arresting, and in many cases, reversing heart disease.
- A varied, well-rounded, plant-based diet, can supply you with all the protein you require. Americans are not lacking in protein at all.
- What Americans are lacking in their diet is fiber. And a fiber deficiency contributes to all sorts of life-threatening illnesses.
- Cancer is not necessarily gene-related. Instead, it is primarily a (mal) nutrition event, a food-borne illness. Indeed, casein (a property in cow milk) has been singled out as the "most relevant chemical carcinogen ever identified".
- The experts also consider heart disease to be a food-borne illness.
- Plants are also a great source for other nutrients besides protein (such as carbohydrates, fats, vitamins, and minerals).
- There are differences between (a) a vegetarian diet; (b) a vegan diet; (c) and a 100%plant-based diet.
- Don't eat junk food or at least eat less junk food.
- Also eating too much animal-based food might cut your life short.
- A good plant-based protein powder is good for you. Make it into a shake and enjoy it along with muffins, brownies, scones and pancakes for a protein-packed meal.
- If you eat more plants and eat less of everything else, you will become healthier, thinner, and live longer.

KNOWLEDGE CHECK

1. Experts have stated that cancer is not necessarily gene-related illness, that instead, it is primarily a (mal) nutrition event, a food-borne illness. Is this true or false? (Check one):

True   [   ]
False   [   ]

2. Experts now also consider heart disease to be a food-borne illness. Is this true or false? (Check one):
True   [ ]
False   [ ]

3. Experts have found that the daily consumption of fruits can decrease the risk of heart disease, stroke and heart attack. Is this true or false? (Check one):
True   [ ]
False   [ ]

4. Besides eating (literally chewing) your vegetables another way you can eat your vegetables is by drinking a vegetable smoothie every day. Is this true or false? (Check one):
True   [ ]
False   [ ]

5. A vegetarian diet will not include meat, poultry, or even fish. Is this true or false? (Check one):
True   [ ]
False   [ ]

6. A vegetarian diet will allow eggs, milk, vegetables and grains Is this true or false? (Check one):
True   [ ]
False   [ ]

7. A vegan diet will not allow meat, fish, poultry, eggs, milk, or honey. But it welcomes vegetables, fruits, grains, and often, over-processed vegan foods Is this true or false? (Check one):
True   [ ]
False   [ ]

8. A 100% plant-based diet allows only 100% plants (that is, grains, vegetables, and fruits). Meat, fish, poultry, eggs, milk, honey, and processed vegan foods are not allowed. Is this true or false? (Check one):
True   [ ]
False   [ ]

9. Junk food is not good for your health. A lot of junk food is filled with sugar, salt, coloring, additives and artificial flavors that confuse the taste buds. If you give up junk food, your taste buds will return to normal and you can taste naturally again. Is this true or false? (Check one):

True   [ ]
False   [ ]

10. Eat less animal-based foods (including meat and cheese). When compared to animal-eaters, vegetarians and vegans were found to have a lower risk of death than animal-eaters. This suggests that eating too much animal-based food decreases longevity. Is this true or false? (Check one):
True   [ ]
False   [ ]

11. By eating more of plants and less of everything else, you will lose unnecessary weight, extend your life span, prevent obesity, reduce the risk of cardiovascular disease, become healthier and lower the risk of death. Is this true or false? (Check one):
True   [ ]
False   [ ]

ACTION STEPS

1. I hereby commit to henceforth eating a plant-based diet. Plants are life and a plant-based diet can be beneficial to me in the following ways:

a. _____

b. _____

c. _____

d. _____

2. It is very easy for me to implement a 100% plant-based diet. To do so I just won't eat any animal product, that is, any food that originates from an animal. Here is a list of animal-based products that I will no longer eat:

a. _____

b. _____

c. _____

d. _____

3. Because you stopped eating meat does not necessarily mean that you can no longer get enough proteins. How do you intend to get enough proteins when you stop eating meat? When I stop eating meat, I will get my proteins from:

a. _____

b. _____

c. _____

d. _____

4. What Americans do not consume enough of, is fiber. Nevertheless, fiber is very important for human health. A deficiency in fiber can lead to a number of illnesses including:

a. _____

b. _____

c. _____

d. _____

5. I will not allow myself to become fiber-deficient. I intend to get enough fiber from the following foods:

a. _____

b. _____

c. _____

d. _____

8. Even as I commit to eating a plant-based diet, I am not worried about how I will get other nutrients (such as carbohydrates, fats, vitamins, and minerals). I will not

allow myself to become deficient in the other nutrients. So, I intend to get enough of these other nutrients from the following foods:

a. _____

b. _____

c. _____

d. _____

9. Being now committed to eating a 100% plant-based diet, the foods I shall eat henceforth will be limited to the following:

a. _____

b. _____

c. _____

d. _____

10. I shall henceforth include **beans and legumes** in my diet. **Beans and legumes** are a great source of the following nutrients:

a. _____

b. _____

c. _____

d. _____

11. I shall also henceforth include a lot of **green** vegetables in my diet. **Green** vegetables are a great source of the following nutrients:

a. _____

b. _____

c. _____

d. _____

12. In addition, I shall henceforth include a lot of **colorful** vegetables in my diet. **Colorful** vegetables are a great source of the following nutrients:

a. _____

b. _____

c. _____

d. _____

13. Some colorful vegetables I love to eat include the following:

a. _____

b. _____

c. _____

d. _____

14. Colorful vegetables can also protect the human body from many diseases including the following:

a. _____

b. _____

c. _____

d. _____

16. I shall also henceforth include a lot of **fruits** in my diet. Fruits are a great source of the following nutrients:

a. _____

b. _____

c. _____

d. _____

18. I shall also henceforth include a lot of **nuts and seeds** in my diet. **Nuts and seeds** are a great source of the following nutrients:

a. _____

b. _____

c. _____

d. _____

19. In addition, I shall henceforth include **whole grains** in my diet. **Whole grains** are a great source of the following nutrients:

a. _____

b. _____

c. _____

d. _____

20. I shall also henceforth include **plant fats (including nut butters and avocados)** in my diet. **Plant fats** are beneficial to the human body in the following ways:

a. _____

b. _____

c. _____

d. _____

CHECKLIST

[ ] Sign the Commitment Certificate (Appendix A), thereby committing myself to eating only a 100% plant-based diet and following all The Greenprint guidelines.

[ ] Avoid animal-based food products including beef, pork, poultry, mutton, fish, milk, cheese, butter, mayonnaise eggs and honey etc.

[ ] Eat enough plants and vegetables every day to meet my daily protein requirement.

[ ] Eat enough plants and vegetables every day to meet my daily fiber requirement.

[ ] Eat enough plants and vegetables everyday to meet my daily requirement for other nutrients, vitamins and minerals.

[ ] Include beans and legumes in my diet.

[ ] Include nuts and seeds in my diet.

[ ] Include whole grains in my diet.

[ ] Include plant fats in my diet.

[ ] Eat a lot of green vegetables every day.

[ ] Eat a lot of colorful vegetables every day.

[ ] Drink a vegetable smoothie every day.

[ ] Eat fruits every day.

[ ] Avoid junk food.

LAW 2: NOBODY EVER PLANS TO FAIL- PEOPLE JUST FAIL TO PLAN

LESSONS

- Develop more sustainable habits that'll make you live longer and look healthier.
- Discard the blame game. Knowing and accepting that you are responsible for what you are today, is the key.
- Be time conscious about your meals, have a good plan and make sure you arrange your meals in measurable proportions of grains, beans, vegetables, legumes, nuts, seeds, and fruits.
- Be a bit more vigilant about the number of nutrients or vitamins your body needs.
- Important nutrients that must be in your diet are: Vitamin B12, Iron, Omega fatty acids, Calcium, Vitamin D, Protein and Zinc.
- Make your daily meals in consonance with the number of vitamins or nutrients your body needs daily to be active and healthy.

KNOWEDGE CHECK

1. When you're switching to plant-based eating, planning is the key for success—and enjoyment! So, set yourself up for success by putting an effort into this goal and planning in detail. When you plan, you win; when you don't plan, you fail. Is this true or false? (Check one):
True   [ ]
False   [ ]

2. The first step to changing the trajectory of your diet, weight, and health is to be completely accountable for where you are today (whether good or bad). You are 100% responsible. You chose what to eat, how to act, where to go, when to exercise (or not), and what foods to avoid. Is this true or false? (Check one):
True   [ ]
False   [ ]

3. The next step is to plan so that a plant-based diet can meet your nutrient needs. It is true that plant foods provide everything you need nutritionally. But ensuring

that you receive all that "everything" requires planning. Is this true or false? (Check one):
True   [ ]
False   [ ]

4. Plant-based eaters have to be a little more vigilant than most to get sufficient amounts of certain vitamins, minerals, and fats in their diets. So, they need to plan their meals around a variety of high-quality, nutrient-rich foods, such as whole grains, beans, legumes, vegetables, fruits, nuts, and seeds. Is this true or false? (Check one):
True   [ ]
False   [ ]

5. A plant-based diet doesn't provide enough iron. Is this true or false? (Check one):
True   [ ]
False   [ ]

6. A plant-based diet doesn't provide enough vitamin B12. Is this true or false? (Check one):
True   [ ]
False   [ ]

7. A plant-based diet doesn't provide enough calcium. Is this true or false? (Check one):
True   [ ]
False   [ ]

8. Studies have shown that avoiding animal-sourced iron (heme iron) and instead sourcing iron from plant food sources (non-heme iron) is associated with a reduced risk of heart disease, diabetes, stroke, and other chronic diseases. Is this true or false? (Check one):
True   [ ]
False   [ ]

ACTION STEPS

9. You need to plan to attain what you want. Therefore, to switch successfully to plant-based eating, I need to anticipate and plan properly for my nutritional needs. I anticipate that my nutritional needs will be as follows:

a. _____

b. _____

c. _____

d. _____

10. I shall meet my above-stated nutritional needs in the following ways:

a. _____

b. _____

c. _____

d. _____

11. To be successful at plant-based eating, I need to make healthy, plant-based foods conveniently available and accessible around me. And I shall achieve this objective in the following ways:

a. _____

b. _____

c. _____

d. _____

12. In order to be able to meet my iron requirements, I shall include the following foods in my plant-based diet:

a. _____

b. _____

c. _____

d. _____

13. In order to be able to meet my vitamin B12 requirements, I shall include the following foods in my plant-based diet:

a. _____

b. _____

c. _____

d. _____

14. In order to be able to meet my Omega-3 fatty acids requirements, I shall include the following foods in my plant-based diet:

a. _____

b. _____

c. _____

d. _____

15. In order to be able to meet my vitamin D requirements, I shall include the following foods in my plant-based diet:

a. _____

b. _____

c. _____

d. _____

16. In order to be able to meet my calcium requirements, I shall include the following foods in my plant-based diet:

a. _____

b. _____

c. _____

d. _____

17. In order to be able to meet my protein requirements, I shall include the following foods in my plant-based diet:

a. _____

b. _____

c. _____

d. _____

18. In order to be able to meet my zinc requirements, I shall include the following foods in my plant-based diet:

a. _____

b. _____

c. _____

d. _____

CHECKLIST

[ ] Plan my switch to plant-based eating.

[ ] Accept that I am 100% responsible for the current state of my health and weight through the diet and lifestyle choices I made in the past.

[ ] Determine my nutritional needs.

[ ] Plan how plant-based diet can meet my nutritional needs

[ ] Plan my meals around a variety of high-quality, nutrient-rich foods, such as whole grains, beans, legumes, vegetables, fruits, nuts, and seeds.

[ ] Ensure that healthy, plant-based food is always conveniently available and accessible around me.

[ ] Ensure that my daily iron requirements are met via my plant-based diet.

[ ] Ensure that my daily Vitamin B-12 requirements are met via my plant-based diet.

[ ] Ensure that my daily Omega-3 fatty acids requirements are met via my plant-based diet.

[ ] Ensure that my daily Vitamin D requirements are met via my plant-based diet.

[ ] Ensure that my daily Calcium requirements are met via my plant-based diet.

[ ] Ensure that my daily Protein requirements are met via my plant-based diet.

[ ] Ensure that my daily Zinc requirements are met via my plant-based diet.

LAW 3: EAT MORE, WEIGH LESS

LESSONS

- Eat simple; eat clean whole foods to become fitter.
- Have a good instructor or support as you journey on your way to fitness and healthy living.
- A change of how you think about yourself and the food you eat is also quite important.
- Plant-based dieting is the most effective way to lose those extra pounds.
- Stop eating over-processed foods; they harm and poison your body.
- It's easy to lose weight, eat more plant-based foods and see that fat melt away.
- You can't gain weight by eating plant-based foods, this is because plant foods have more nutrients and less calories.
- The contributory factor for a healthy weight-loss through eating plant foods is "fiber".
- Fiber has been known to cure many devastating diseases.
- Steak isn't Fiber!

KNOWLEDGE CHECK

1. The starting point to having a healthy weight loss is to have good mental discipline. Is this true or false? (Check one):
True   [ ]
False   [ ]

2. The great thing about eating plant foods, is that you do not have to stop eating so you can lose weight. With plant-based eating, you can eat as much as you want and still look healthy and fit. Is this true or false? (Check one):
True   [ ]
False   [ ]

3. A plant-based diet also comes with a high fiber content which has so many benefits for the body. Is this true or false? (Check one):
True   [ ]
False   [ ]

4. A plant-based diet also comes with A high fiber content which has so many benefits for the body. Is this true or false? (Check one):
True   [ ]
False   [ ]

5. Regarding the United States, a USDA dietary report has stated that 97% of Americans lack fiber. Is this true or false? (Check one):
True   [ ]
False   [ ]

6. Fiber can be found in steak. Is this true or false? (Check one):
True   [ ]
False   [ ]

7. Fiber can only be found in plant and nowhere else. Is this true or false? (Check one):
True   [ ]
False   [ ]

8. There are two types of fiber, and they are; insoluble and soluble fiber. Soluble fiber extracts calories and toxins from the body, while insoluble fiber discards or removes toxins from the body as the insoluble fiber passes through the digestive tract. Is this true or false? (Check one):
True   [ ]
False   [ ]

9. By eating a plant-based diet you'll become fitter and thinner. Vegans have been found to be slimmer and fitter than all categories of food eaters, be it vegetarians or the meat and fish eaters. Is this true or false? (Check one):
True   [ ]
False   [ ]

10. Plant foods do not have to be eaten only for weight loss. They can also be eaten to prevent many terminal or life-threatening diseases. Is this true or false? (Check one):
True   [ ]
False   [ ]

ACTION STEPS

1. The starting point to having a healthy weight loss and achieving good health is to have good mental discipline. I hereby commit to training my mind and improving my mental discipline by doing the following mind-training exercises everyday:

a. _____

b. _____

c. _____

d. _____

2. On this journey I will surround myself with support. I will surround myself with like minds who will encourage me and assist me, including the following persons:

a. _____

b. _____

c. _____

d. _____

3. On this journey I will also regularly consult with and follow the directives of a diet instructor. I will research and choose a diet instructor to work with from among the following diet instructors:

a. _____

b. _____

c. _____

d. _____

3. Regular exercise is also essential for an effective weight loss and overall good-health-achievement program. I hereby commit to exercising at least four days per week. My weekly four-day exercise plan is as follows:

a. _____

b. _____

c. _____

d. _____

3. A plant-based diet can prevent a lot of life-threatening diseases. I hereby commit to eating a plant-based diet so I can prevent the following diseases that are of concern to me:

a. _____

b. _____

c. _____

d. _____

Both soluble and insoluble fiber have been found to affect our body in various ways including the following:

a. _____

b. _____

c. _____

d. _____

CHECKLIST

[ ] Engage in daily mind-training exercises so I can train my mind and improve my mental discipline.

[ ] Engage in physical training exercises at least four days every week.

[ ] Retain a good instructor to guide me on my way to fitness, weight loss and healthy living.

[ ] Surround myself with like-minded persons who will encourage me and assist me on my journey to fitness, weight loss and healthy living.

[ ] Eat only simple, clean, whole plant-based foods. Do not eat over-processed foods.

[ ] Ensure that I get a good dose of fiber, daily, through eating a plant-based diet.

[ ] Change how I think of myself and the food that I eat. Use food to achieve fitness, weight loss and healthy living, and to prevent and beat disease.

LAW 4: WATER IS LIFE FUEL

LESSONS

- Water is the fuel of life.
- Water which makes up 70% of your body is highly essential for the maintenance of your body system.
- Water helps in circulation and metabolism.
- Water helps the body to also metabolize stored fats.
- Water energizes and can provide full feeling even before a meal.
- When you convert to plant-based eating, you need to drink more water, because fiber absorbs a lot of water.
- Water is a basic component for brain metabolism. You need water to develop a more active brain.
- Water has also been found to prevent benign and malignant cancers.
- Water flushes out toxins or harmful wastes from your body.
- Water also makes you look young and vibrant and gives you that youthful glow.
- Do eat plenty fruits and vegetables (watermelons, mangoes, oranges, grapes, pineapples, cucumbers, apples, carrots, tomatoes, etc.). Fruits contain a large percentage of water.
- On average, men should drink thirteen 8-ounce cups of water daily, and women should drink nine 8-ounce cups of water daily.

KNOWLEDGE CHECK

1. Water helps in maintaining your body's metabolic rate and activates the enzymes in your body to break down nutrients like glucose, protein, fats and starches. Is this true or false? (Check one):
True   [   ]
False   [   ]

2. Water does not help to dilute stored fats in the body. It is also not a medium for the effective distribution of nutrients throughout your body. Is this true or false? (Check one):
True   [   ]
False   [   ]

3. Water does not make up the bulk of the grease in your joints, called synovial fluid. It also does not make up the bulk of the cerebrospinal fluid, found in your spine, and in between the vertebra. Water also does not make up the bulk of the

fluid found in all your other organs, muscles, brain, cells and even your DNA. Is this true or false? (Check one):
True   [ ]
False   [ ]

4. Regular intake of water can prevent cancerous growths and urinary tract diseases. Is this true or false? (Check one):
True   [ ]
False   [ ]

5. Dehydration is like an alarm or warning call from your body stating that it needs fuel without which all body activities slow down. Is this true or false? (Check one):
True   [ ]
False   [ ]

6. Plant-based foods contain an overwhelming amount of fiber. When you ingest fiber from your meals, without drinking enough water, it could cause you constipation. So, you need to drink lots of water if you are on a plant-based diet. Is this true or false? (Check one):
True   [ ]
False   [ ]

7. Succulent fruits such as melons, grapes, oranges, watermelon, apples, cannot help you to meet your daily water requirement and eating at least five servings of fruits and vegetables daily cannot supply your body with 20% of your daily water requirement. Is this true or false? (Check one):
True   [ ]
False   [ ]

ACTION STEPS

1. Since I have committed myself to eating a 100% plant-based diet, and since plant-based foods contain a large quantity of fiber, thus requiring me to drink lots of water, I hereby also commit to drinking an adequate quantity of water daily in accordance with the average daily water requirements for men and women which are as follows:

a. _____

b. _____

c. _____

d. _____

2. In order to avoid dehydration, I shall always check the water level in my body by conducting the Body-Water-Level Self-Test upon myself. The Body-Water-Level Self-Test is conducted as follows (also indicate the meaning of colorless urine and "lemonade-looking" urine):

a. _____

b. _____

c. _____

d. _____

CHECKLIST

[ ] FOR A MAN: drink at least thirteen 8-ounce cups of water, daily. FOR A WOMAN: drink at least nine 8-ounce cups of water, daily.

[ ] Eat plenty of fruits and vegetables. Succulent fruits, particularly, contain a large percentage of water.

[ ] Eat at least five servings of fruits and vegetables daily. This can supply my body with 20% of my daily water requirement.

[ ] Conduct the Body-Water-Level Self-Test upon myself regularly, in order to detect and avoid dehydration.

LAW 5: PROTECT YOUR HEART

LESSONS

- Your heart is your life.
- Risk to the heart begins almost when a person is born.
- To avoid heart-related ailments, exercise regularly and eat more plant-based foods.
- Plant-based eating is the most effective way or lifestyle to reverse heart diseases.
- Have a diet mixed with whole grains, vegetables, nuts, legumes and fruits. Insist on eating only plant-based foods to have a healthy heart.
- Eating too much of meat can increase the risk of death. Meat shortens longevity.
- Meat strains the heart.

KNOWLEDGE CHECK

1. One's lifestyle will ultimately affect the functioning and health of one's heart. When the heart develops an issue or ceases altogether, it is usually as a result of lifestyle-induced abuse. Is this true or false? (Check one):
True   [ ]
False   [ ]

2. The consumption of junk food and meat has been found and confirmed to not be the major cause of various heart-related diseases. Is this true or false? (Check one):
True   [ ]
False   [ ]

3. Eating a strictly 100% plant-based diet and exercising regularly can prevent heart disease. Is this true or false? (Check one):
True   [ ]
False   [ ]

4. Eating four or five servings of fruits and vegetables a day does not decrease (but instead increases) the risk of having a heart disease by 17%. Is this true or false? (Check one):
True   [ ]

False   [ ]

5. It is never too late to make changes to one's lifestyle and to begin to eat a plant-based diet and exercise regularly in order to lose weight and improve one's fitness and overall health status. Right now, is a good time to make the lifestyle change. Is this true or false? (Check one):
True   [ ]
False   [ ]

ACTION STEPS

1. My lifestyle and diet habits will ultimately affect the functioning and health of my heart. Some of my negative lifestyle and diet habits which I hereby pledge to change or discard altogether, include the following:
a. _____

b. _____

c. _____

d. _____

2. I will henceforth abstain from eating junk food and meat. And the reasons why I will do so are as follows:
a. _____

b. _____

c. _____

d. _____

3. Eating a strictly 100% plant-based diet is also essential for heart health and can help prevent heart disease. I therefore commit to following a 100% plant-based diet. And my plans to ensure that healthy, plant-based food is always conveniently available and accessible around me, is as follows:
a. _____

b. _____

c. _____

d. _____

4. Regular exercise is also essential for heart health and can help prevent heart disease. So, I hereby commit to exercising at least four days per week. My weekly four-day exercise plan is as follows:

a. _____

b. _____

c. _____

d. _____

5. I shall eat four or five servings of fruits and vegetables every day, as doing so decreases my risk of having a heart disease by 17%. And my plans to ensure that I eat four or five servings of fruits and vegetables every day, is as follows:

a. _____

b. _____

c. _____

d. _____

CHECKLIST

[ ] Discard all my lifestyle and diet habits which can negatively affect my heart.

[ ] Abstain from eating junk food and meat.

[ ] Eat a strictly 100% plant-based diet, daily.

[ ] Eat four or five servings of fruits and vegetables daily.

[ ] Exercise at least four days per week.

LAW 6: TAKE CARE OF YOUR MIND

LESSONS

- Plant-based eating facilitates brain activity.
- Plant-based eating prevents neurodegenerative diseases such as, Alzheimer.
- There are so many God-given plants that help in reducing the menace of brain diseases, as they contain sufficient neuro-protective nutrients.
- Saturated fat, found in meat-based diets blocks the blood vessels of the brain, thereby triggering intense inflammation.
- What you eat is the basis of how healthy and long you'll live.
- To protect your brain against dementia and other brain-related diseases, make sure to eat plenty of legumes, vegetables, fresh fruits and vegetables.
- Eat foods high in polyphenols. This is a type of antioxidant that tends to concentrate in the brain. It can only be found in plants.
- Make a choice to only eat plant-based meals. Make it a habit. This habit will protect you from various diseases that are detrimental to health. Plants are life. Eat more vegetables. Also eat plenty of fruits, beans, legumes, seeds, nuts, and whole grains.

KNOWLEDGE CHECK

1. Following a plant-based diet has zero beneficial effects on the brain or mind. A plant-based diet does not enhance cognitive capabilities enabling one to become more accurate, focused and alert. And a plant-based diet does not help one's body to prevent or beat brain diseases). Is this true or false? (Check one):
True [ ]
False [ ]

2. Foods high in saturated fats are dangerous to the brain as well as the heart). Is this true or false? (Check one):
True [ ]
False [ ]

3. Saturated fats can block the blood vessels in the brain, thus triggering inflammation in the brain and preventing the brain from intaking a particular protein that helps to protect the brain from beta-amyloid plaque (a starter for Alzheimer's disease). Is this true or false? (Check one):
True [ ]
False [ ]

4. Following a 100% plant-based diet can protect your brain from the risk of dementia and other degenerative brain diseases). Is this true or false? (Check one):
True [ ]
False [ ]

5. Plant-based foods are rich in polyphenols (a kind of antioxidant that fights chronic inflammation). Polyphenols also tend to concentrate more in the brain, thereby lowering the risk of age-related brain diseases. Is this true or false? (Check one):
True [ ]
False [ ]

ACTION STEPS

1. Foods high in saturated fats are dangerous to the brain as well as the heart. Explain how this is so and draw a list of all the sources of saturated fats that you consume:

a. _____

b. _____

c. _____

d. _____

2. A plant-based diet is very beneficial to the brain or mind. Explain the many ways in which this is so.

a. _____

b. _____

c. _____

d. _____

3. Polyphenols are a kind of antioxidant that fights chronic inflammation. They tend to concentrate more in the brain. I intend to get my daily dose of polyphenols through the following means:

a. _____

b. _____

c. _____

d. _____

CHECKLIST

[ ] Stay committed to a strictly 100% plant-based diet. Never give up!

[ ] Avoid foods that contain saturated fats.

[ ] Avoid eating meat.

[ ] Eat plant-based foods that are high in polyphenols.

LAW 7: FAST FOR HEALTH AND LONGETIVITY

LESSONS

- Sleeping is a kind of intermittent fasting.
- Intermittent fasting sheds a large proportion, approximately 80% to 100% of pure fats.
- Intermittent fasting has been found to make us live longer, according to researchers.
- Intermittent fasting also helps in autophagy which is a mechanism or process by which the cells in our body clean themselves and disassemble any dysfunctional or unnecessary parts. Without autophagy, our cells will become damaged and cease to function properly or cease to function at all.
- Intermittent fasting helps in maintaining your blood sugar.
- Intermittent fasting maintains your digestive tracts by triggering important cell repairing processes, thereby preventing inflammation.
- Intermittent fasting helps your body to be at its optimal state by making you consume fewer calories, thereby you lose belly fat and a few pounds of weight.
- Intermittent fasting has been found to speed up metabolic activities.
- It activates and stimulates your brain, by fostering the growth of brain cells.
- It strengthens your body's immune system, by boosting the production of more white blood cells that help to fight bacteria, viruses or infections.
- It also makes you look younger, i.e., giving an anti-aging effect to your body.

KNOWLEDGE CHECK

1. Intermittent fasting is basically an eating pattern, in which you alternate or switch between periods of eating and fasting. Is this true or false? (Check one):
True [   ]
False [   ]

2. Intermittent fasting alters one's mitochondria, thereby slowing the process of aging and ultimately improves one's health. Is this true or false? (Check one):
True [   ]
False [   ]

3. Intermittent fasting has also been found to support the process of autophagy – a cell-cleaning mechanism which our cell automatically undertakes. Is this true or false? (Check one):
True [ ]
False [ ]

4. Intermittent fasting can induce weight loss very effectively. Typically, it can induce weight loss of between 7 to 11 pounds within a period of ten weeks. Is this true or false? (Check one):
True [ ]
False [ ]

ACTION STEPS

1. Intermittent fasting is beneficial to my health in the following ways:

a. _____

b. _____

c. _____

d. _____

2. Intermittent fasting is beneficial to my health and I intend to include it in my new lifestyle and dietary change program in the following ways:

a. _____

b. _____

c. _____

d. _____

CHECKLIST

[ ] Include intermittent fasting in my new lifestyle and dietary change program.

[ ] Get adequate sleep every day. Sleeping is a kind of intermittent fasting which is good for me in many ways. An adult needs between 7 to 9 hours of sleep every night.

LAW 8: THINK ABOUT THE EARTH BEFORE YOU EAT

LESSONS

- Western foods or diets have been found to be particularly unhealthy.
- Most foods that you buy in a store, was made for you, but passed the process of degrading the environment where you live or in some other place.
- The best catch in sustaining the environment is by eating foods that are locally grown around your vicinity. This is what is called "Locavore".
- Being a locavore helps to reduce the energy consumed in producing food, thereby decreasing greenhouse emissions.
- Locally grown food has been found to be healthier than processed foods.
- Locally grown food tastes better and has more retention of its nutrients.
- A good way of growing your organic food is by growing it on your own, perhaps at your backyard or growing your crops by using a container garden.
- Growing your food at home, saves a whole lot of cash.
- Planting your seed and watching it blossom, makes you to appreciate your environment. You become more environmentally-inclined.

KNOWLEDGE CHECK

1. Western diets are now known to be unhealthy and degrading to the environment. Is this true or false? (Check one):
True [ ]
False [ ]

2. Many present day agricultural and farming practices damage the soil and contaminate our natural habitats. Is this true or false? (Check one):
True [ ]
False [ ]

3. Packaged or processed foods tend to use much more energy (in their production) than whole foods. Packaged or processed foods also contribute to packaging waste. And they do not in conform with fitness and health goals. Is this true or false? (Check one):
True [ ]

False [ ]

4. A locavore is someone who buys and eats only locally grown foods. Is this true or false? (Check one):
True [ ]
False [ ]

ACTION STEPS

1. My lifestyle and diet choices impact both my health and the environment in the following ways:

a. _____

b. _____

c. _____

d. _____

2. The following are some sustainable food habits which I will cultivate and which I believe will translate into huge differences for me and for the environment:

a. _____

b. _____

c. _____

d. _____

3. The following are some of the ways I and the environment can benefit if I buy and eat only locally grown foods:

a. _____

b. _____

c. _____

d. _____

4. The following are some of the ways that I and the environment will benefit if I avoid hoarding and shopping in too much bulk and only buy food and produce for the short term):

a. _____

b. _____

c. _____

d. _____

5. I have other environment-friendly ideas which I believe will help me to leave the smallest carbon foot-print in my daily activities. These ideas include the following:

a. _____

b. _____

c. _____

d. _____

CHECKLIST

[ ] Make lifestyle and diet choices that positively impact both my health and the environment.

[ ] Cultivate important and sustainable food habits that can translate into huge differences.

[ ] Become a locavore. Buy and eat only locally grown foods.

[ ] Plan my weekly menus and buy only as much food or produce as I will need for the short term. Do not hoard items or buy in too much bulk because that often leads to waste.

[ ] Choose whole foods over packaged or processed foods.

[ ] Think about the earth before I eat. Doing so will make me more environment-friendly. It will also motivate me to leave the smallest carbon foot-print.

LAW 9: LOVE FOOD THAT LOVES YOU BACK

LESSONS

- Eat only those foods that love you, that improve your health and enhance your longevity.
- You can train your taste buds to adjust to the kind of foods you eat. The taste buds adjust quickly to change.
- To train your kids' taste buds to enjoy only plant-based foods, feed your kids with vegetables, grains, beans, lentils, fruits, nuts and seeds.
- Patronize only foods that you love, which in turn loves you and the planet back. Flee from processed foods. They are your worst enemies.

KNOWLEDGE CHECK

1. Food does not have any health consequences at all (either good or bad). Is this true or false? (Check one):
True [   ]
False [   ]

2. The nutrient-rich, healthy foods that love you, improve your health and enhance your vitality are predominantly plant-based foods. Is this true or false? (Check one):
True [   ]
False [   ]

3. Processed foods, junk food, and sweet foods love you. They are good for your health. Is this true or false? (Check one):
True [   ]
False [   ]

4. The taste buds easily yield to changes. Your taste buds can adjust to new tastes very quickly. If your taste buds are, for now, accustomed to junk foods, processed foods or sweet foods, you can retrain them to begin to like the taste of plant-based foods. It is not too late for you to retrain your taste buds. And right now, is the right time to start. Is this true or false? (Check one):
True [   ]
False [   ]

5. In as little as two weeks, your taste buds can become accustomed to the food you introduce to it. Is this true or false? (Check one):
True [ ]
False [ ]

6. Children should not be allowed to reject healthy foods. Continuously offer healthy foods to them. With time they'll get used to eating healthy foods. This will greatly prepare them for healthy future. Is this true or false? (Check one):
True [ ]
False [ ]

7. According to researchers, individuals who eat a predominantly plant-based diet (such as vegetarians and vegans) enjoy a lower risk of death from heart disease, obesity and other ailments, as compared to meat eaters. Is this true or false? (Check one):
True [ ]
False [ ]

ACTION STEPS

1. The following are some of the foods that love me and that I will begin to eat or continue to eat to improve my health and enhance my longevity:

a. _____

b. _____

c. _____

d. _____

2. The following are some of the foods that hate me and wish me ill. I will avoid eating or discontinue eating these foods so as not to damage my health and reduce my longevity:

a. _____

b. _____

c. _____

d. _____

3. I will train my kids to accept and enjoy plant-based foods. I will persistently offer them plant-based foods such as vegetables, grains, beans, lentils, fruits, nuts and seeds. In the event that they resist or reject these foods, I will strategically handle that situation in the following ways:

a. _____

b. _____

c. _____

d. _____

CHECKLIST

[ ] Search for and eat only foods that love me. These are the nutrient-rich, healthy, plant-based foods that will improve my health and enhance my longevity.

[ ] Avoid processed foods, sweet foods, and junk food. These are foods that hate me and wish me ill.

[ ] Train my taste buds to love plant-based foods. It's easy. My taste buds can adjust to plant-based foods in only as little as 2 weeks.

[ ] Train my kids not to reject healthy foods. Consistently offer them plant-based foods. Be persistent. With time they'll get used to it.

LAW 10: MOVEMENT BEGETS MOVEMENT

LESSONS

- The more you exercise, the more active you become. The more active we become, the better you feel about yourself and the better you feel about yourself, the more things or goals you can accomplish.
- Make time to do something physical every day, like walking or jogging.
- Make exercising a habit, by including it in your daily schedule.
- Maintain your momentum in keeping up with your exercise habit. The more you move, the more your health will improve.
- You start losing about 1% of your strength per year from age fifty. To prevent this from happening to you or to reverse it if it is already happening to you, begin doing and persist with weight training and resistance exercises. Don't give up!

KNOWLEDGE CHECK

1. The aging population should go to the gym even more than young people. This is because weight training helps to prevent muscular atrophy (wasting away of the muscles). Is this true or false? (Check one):
True [　]
False [　]

2. It has been found that a person begins to lose 1 % of strength per year around the age of fifty. This is therefore a good reason to keep on engaging in your resistance-training routine so as to lower your risk of developing osteoarthritis or osteoporosis. Is this true or false? (Check one):
True [　]
False [　]

3. Exercise is not important for your body. It does not improve brain activity and it does not enhance the functioning of your heart. It also does not lower your cholesterol levels and it does not reduce your risk of developing some cancerous growth. Is this true or false? (Check one):
True [　]
False [　]

4. According to research, exercising for 150 to 450 minutes per week reduces one's risk of premature death by 39%. Is this true or false? (Check one):

True [ ]
False [ ]

ACTION STEPS

1. Motivation is essential to start and stick to a fitness, weight loss and good health program and to plant-based eating. To keep myself motivated as I move forward, I will do the following:

a. _____

b. _____

c. _____

d. _____

2. A sedentary lifestyle is dangerous. And it is very important to do something physical every day. So, I hereby commit to engaging in the following physical activities every day for at least 20 minutes per day:

a. _____

b. _____

c. _____

d. _____

CHECKLIST

[ ] Do something physical every day, like walking or jogging, etc. A sedentary lifestyle is dangerous.

[ ] Include exercising in my daily routine. Make exercising a habit. Exercise daily.

[ ] Motivation is essential! Maintain my motivation and momentum in my exercise habit. Stick to it! Do not give up! It gets easier with time.

[ ] Engage in weight training and resistance exercises to gain and maintain strength and to help prevent muscular atrophy (wasting away of the muscles), and to lower the risk of developing osteoarthritis or osteoporosis.

LAW 11: TRASH MUST BE TAKEN OUT

LESSONS

- You can strengthen your body's detoxification levels by eating plant-based foods.
- Our body organs have been naturally detoxifying waste products from our system since we were born.
- Detoxification is all about dislodging toxins and eventually eliminating them from our body so as to prevent further harm.
- Detoxification improves the way you look, think and reduces the signs of aging.
- Plant-based foods are the best detoxifying agents.
- Plant-based foods are also effective antioxidants.
- Water is also a very good detoxifying agent. Gods own "medicinal syrup".
- When you drink water, it helps to flush out toxins from your body through urine and sweat. Yes, sweating is a kind of detoxification.

KNOWLEDGE CHECK

1. Detoxification is natural. Our body naturally detoxifies waste and toxins from our system through our various organs. But when waste and toxins are allowed to linger in your body, they can become dangerous. Toxins are known to change into free radicals if they are allowed to linger for too long in the body without being dislodged and eliminated. Is this true or false? (Check one):
True [   ]
False [   ]

2. The only natural way to enhance the effectiveness of the detoxification process is to eat plant-based foods. Eating plant-based foods quickens the waste elimination process while at the same time it benefits your body in many other ways (e.g. improving your looks, enhancing your brain functions, eliminating allergic reactions, supporting weight reduction and slowing the aging process). Is this true or false? (Check one):
True [   ]
False [   ]

3. Plant-based foods are not rich in antioxidants. And antioxidants do not help to eliminate free radicals from our body system. Is this true or false? (Check one):
True [ ]
False [ ]

4. Some of the best detoxifiers include: garlic and onions; liver-friendly foods like brans, apples, legumes, carrots, and dandelions etc.; vegetables; high-fiber foods, beets, cruciferous vegetables, and flavonoid-rich foods such as fruits, berries, etc. Is this true or false? (Check one):
True [ ]
False [ ]

5. A scientific study which examined urine samples had found that people who consume processed food had a larger dose of toxins in their bodies than people who do not eat processed foods. Is this true or false? (Check one):
True [ ]
False [ ]

ACTION STEPS

1. The following are some of the processed and animal-based foods that I must avoid eating or discontinue eating because they could introduce toxins into my body:

a. _____

b. _____

c. _____

d. _____

2. Drinking water is a major means of detoxifying my body. I therefore hereby commit to drinking an adequate quantity of water daily in accordance with the average daily water requirements for men and women which are as follows:

a. _____

b. _____

c. _____

d. _____

3. The following are some of the plant-based foods that can strengthen my body's detoxification system; and some antioxidant-rich foods that can protect my body against tissue damage and free radicals. And I hereby commit to begin to eat them or to continue to eat them so as to improve my health and enhance my longevity:

a. _____

b. _____

c. _____

d. _____

CHECKLIST

[ ] Be more cautious about processed and animal-based foods. They introduce a higher percentage of toxins into our body.

[ ] Drinking water is also another means of achieving detoxification. A glass of water can flush out a mass of toxins through sweat and urine.

[ ] Eat plant-based foods to strengthen the body's detoxification system.

[ ] Consume antioxidant-rich foods to protect yourself against tissue damage which may result from free radicals in the body.

LAW 12: THE WORLD DOESN'T NEED US TO SURVIVE – WE NEED THE WORLD TO SURVIVE

LESSONS

- Plant-based diets are better for the planet than animal-based diets.
- Animal farming is inflicting damage on the earth in a large scale.
- Eating meat has been found to create food shortages. This is because crops are used to feed livestock.
- Overfishing is known to threaten the existence of many fish species.
- Fish farming pollutes rivers and other fresh-water bodies.
- Farm animals are subjected to the cruelest treatments in slaughterhouses.
- Farm animals are injected with chemicals and hormones to make them grow bigger and faster. And this in turn, is sold to us to eat.
- Physiologically our bodies were made to eat vegetables and fruits, not animals.
- The little things you do matter in your relationship to the earth. For example, how you transport yourself, what you eat, what kind of clothes you buy, etc. are all important in terms of their impact upon the environment.
- Do not underestimate the power of the impact of your very own habits. Just one sustainable habit that you practice can ultimately change the entire food system and stabilize the world.

KNOWLEDGE CHECK

1. Our eating habit affects our planet greatly. By eating only plant-based foods, you're being a partaker of sustainability, thereby solving the issues of environmental degradation in our planet. Is this true or false? (Check one):
True [   ]
False [   ]

2. The meat that people eat consumes a great deal of energy and environmental resources for their production. This, in turn, wreaks havoc on our environment. Mounting evidence suggests that every step of meat production, beginning with the feeding of the animals all the way down to the refining of meat, depletes our

natural resources and inflicts severe damages to our environment. Is this true or false? (Check one):
True [   ]
False [   ]

3. Methane is a huge contributor to global warming. It is even more potent in trapping heat than carbon dioxide. And now it is estimated that animal farming (rearing animals to be killed for meat) emits over 100 million tons of methane gas into the atmosphere per year. In fact, animal farming has been tagged the major contributor to climate change, discharging more gaseous wastes than ships, planes or cars the world over. Is this true or false? (Check one):
True [   ]
False [   ]

4. Carbon dioxide is another greenhouse gas that is being unleashed into the atmosphere due to human activities. In fact, eating a hamburger causes about the same rate of damage to the atmosphere as driving your car for a three-week period. Is this true or false? (Check one):
True [   ]
False [   ]

5. Physiologically our bodies were designed by God to eat mostly meat instead of vegetables and fruits. Is this true or false? (Check one):
True [   ]
False [   ]

6. Humans have pointed teeth and comparatively short intestines that are shorter than our bodies and that can easily break down meat in our systems. This is because God designed humans to eat mostly meat, to be carnivores. I am, therefore, a proud carnivore! Is this true or false? (Check one):
True [   ]
False [   ]

7. Assuming you (and other members of your family) were to avoid meat and other animal-based products and instead follow a 100% plant-based diet, you all would ultimately save the lives of approximately 200 animals every year. Is this true or false? (Check one):
True [   ]
False [   ]

8. The typical American diet is meat heavy. And experts have warned that if everyone on earth ate the same diet as the typical, meat-heavy American diet, that by the year 2050, the population of the earth at that time would require approximately 3.74 earths to accommodate and sustain it. Is this true or false? (Check one):
True [ ]
False [ ]

ACTION STEPS

1. Carbon dioxide is a greenhouse gas that is unleashed into the atmosphere due to human activities. Indeed, eating a hamburger causes about the same rate of damage to the atmosphere as driving your car for a three-week period. Explain how this is so. And in your answer, indicate the average emission of carbon dioxide from a typical car per day (and then for three weeks) compared to the average emission of carbon dioxide from the process of producing a single burger:

a. _____

b. _____

c. _____

d. _____

2. If you are so moved, indicate here in writing that, henceforth, you will no longer consume hamburgers or other processed meat products. Also indicate other measures you will henceforth take to protect our environment reduce your carbon footprint and protect your health (Note: if you are not so moved, then kindly move on to the next question).

a. _____

b. _____

c. _____

d. _____

3. On the other hand, if you think that this is all bullcrap, please indicate that here in writing. Also state in writing that you will continue to eat hamburgers and other processed meat products as much as you darn please. Also indicate other measures you will continue to engage in to harm and pollute our environment, increase your carbon footprint and destroy your health.

    a. _____

    b. _____

    c. _____

    d. _____

4. Eating meat has been found to create food shortages. In fact, if more people were to follow a plant-based diet (instead of consuming so much meat), there would be more food available, globally, than there currently is. Explain how animal farming and meat consumption cause food shortages:

    a. _____

    b. _____

    c. _____

    d. _____

5. Explain your plan to quit eating meat and instead follow a plant-based diet. Also explain how plan to influence those close to you to also quit eating meat and instead follow a plant-based diet.

    a. _____

    b. _____

    c. _____

    d. _____

CHECKLIST

[ ] Remind at least one person each day that plant-based diets are better for the planet than animal-based diets.

[ ] Remind at least one person each day that animal farming is inflicting damage on the earth on a large scale.

[ ] Remember that physiologically the human body (including mine) was made to eat vegetables and fruits, not animals.

[ ] Do not to underestimate the power of the impact of my choices and habits upon the environment. So, in my daily choices of how I transport myself, what I eat, what kind of clothes I buy, etc., I will be wise and consider my health and the heath of the environment. Indeed, the daily choices I make and habits I practice can ultimately change the entire food system and stabilize the world.

[ ] Eat only plant-based foods. The foods we choose to eat affect not only us but also the environment and our planet both positively and negatively.

[ ] Avoid eating hamburgers, meat generally and other processed animal-based food products.

[ ] Also avoid eating the typical meat-heavy American diet. Eat only plant-based foods.

[ ] Take other measures on my own initiative to protect the environment, reduce my carbon footprint and protect my health.

[ ] Influence my family members and those close to me to eat only plant-based foods; to avoid eating hamburgers, meat generally and other processed animal-based food products; to avoid eating the typical meat-heavy American diet; and to take other measures on their own initiative to protect the environment, reduce their carbon footprint and protect their health.

LAW 13: CHANGE STARTS WITH YOU

LESSONS

- The change you seek starts with you.
- We have to always examine our habits to know where we have to make a change.
- Make good food choices. Good food choices are good for our health and the health of our planet.
- Go for the things that matter when buying food stuff. This is done by scaling back on your budget.
- Have a good Greenprint for the way you cook, how you store food and how you dispose of your waste, etc.
- Use energy-efficient technologies; they are sold cheaply in the market. By using them, you save a great deal on electricity or power.
- Set your appliances in the most appropriate and minimal manner. This can save you lot on power.
- Prepare your own meals, instead of buying fast food. This is beneficial for your own health.

KNOWLEDGE CHECK

1. Everything we ever do as humans, all our daily activities, have an impact on the environment. So, it's important we take notice of our choices, habits, and lifestyle in terms of their impact on the environment. Is this true or false? (Check one):
True [ ]
False [ ]

2. The carbon dioxide we emit contributes to global warming and climate change. Is this true or false? (Check one):
True [ ]
False [ ]

3. Reducing your consumption of meat can reduce your environmental footprint to less than half the amount it currently is. Is this true or false? (Check one):
True [ ]
False [ ]

4. Energy-efficient technologies are affordable and available. They can help you maintain power production in the most efficient manner, and help to reduce the effects of global-warming on our planet by 1%-2%. Is this true or false? (Check one):
True [ ]
False [ ]

5. Preparing your meals by yourself instead of buying fast food, in the long run, will significantly benefit your health. Is this true or false? (Check one):
True [ ]
False [ ]

6. As a consumer, you call the shots on companies' production practices. You vote with your money. If a company maintains unsustainable food production practices, you can show your disapproval by simply not buying their products. It's that simple. You don't necessarily need to lobby Congress to make your point. You can use your purchasing power to better the planet. Is this true or false? (Check one):
True [ ]
False [ ]

7. Eaters of plant-based foods generate about 1.1 tons of carbon dioxide **PER YEAR**, while meat eaters produce about 2.8 tons of carbon dioxide **EVERY DAY**! Is this true or false? (Check one):
True [ ]
False [ ]

8. The change the planet needs can start with you. For example, if you decided to avoid eating meat and processed foods, that decision would immediately and tremendously reduce your carbon foot print and that is good for the environment. Is this true or false? (Check one):
True [ ]
False [ ]

ACTION STEPS

1. The change to make our planet greener and cleaner and our bodies healthier starts with you. Write down what you understand by this statement? Also write what your plans are for your own personal role in starting the change and making our environment and the planet better?

   a. _____

   b. _____

c. _____

d. _____

2. Write down those habits and choices of yours that you need to change in order to help better our environment and planet.

a. _____

b. _____

c. _____

d. _____

3. Write down how you plan to better your food choices so as to better your heath and the health of our environment.

a. _____

b. _____

c. _____

d. _____

4. Write down how you plan to purchase only necessary commodities in limited quantities so as to avoid unnecessary waste. Make references to the budgeting modifications that you intend to make so you can achieve this goal.

a. _____

b. _____

c. _____

d. _____

5. Write down your Greenprint plan for how you intend to alter the way you cook, the way you store your food and the way you dispose of your waste, so that they can all be environmentally friendly.

a. _____

b. _____

c. _____

d. _____

6. Energy efficient technologies are good for the environment. Write down your plan of how you intend to include the use of energy-efficient technologies in your use of electricity.

a. _____

b. _____

c. _____

d. _____

7. Preparing your own meals (instead of buying fast food) is beneficial for your own health. Explain why this is so. Also write down a sustainable plan for henceforth preparing your own food by yourself.

a. _____

b. _____

c. _____

d. _____

8. Articulate a sustainable plan of how you intend to quit eating meat and processed foods.

a. _____

b. _____

c. _____

d. _____

9. As a consumer, you can use your purchasing power to better the planet by refusing to patronize companies whose production practices are questionable or unsustainable. Write down the companies and products you are considering boycotting and explain why you are considering boycotting them. Be sure to explain how their practices are unsustainable and unfriendly to the environment. Also explain whether or not you have notified them to change their unsustainable practices and given them a reasonable opportunity to make the change.

a. _____

b. _____

c. _____

d. _____

CHECKLIST

[ ] I understand that the change the planet needs starts with me.

[ ] Examine my habits, choices and lifestyle on a daily basis to determine where I have to make a change.

[ ] Make good food choices every day. Basically, eat only plant-based foods.

[ ] Scale back on my food and produce budget and buy only things that are necessary and in limited quantity

[ ] Conduct a daily examination to ensure that the way I cook, the way I store my food and the way I dispose of my waste, etc., are all environmentally friendly.

[ ] Begin to use energy-efficient technologies immediately.

[ ] Begin to set my appliances appropriately so that they can use minimal power. Also turn off my appliances that are not in use so I can save on power. Begin this immediately.

[ ] Prepare my own meals. Avoid buying fast food. This is beneficial for my health.

[ ] Do not eat meat, animal-based food products and processed foods.

[ ] Use my money, my purchasing power to better the planet. Do not patronize companies and products that maintain unsustainable and environmentally unfriendly practices.

[ ] Always think of new and creative ways to reduce my environmental footprint.

[ ] Remind at least one person each day that the change our planet needs starts with each of us, personally.

LAW 14: THE BEST STARTING POINT IS TODAY

LESSONS

- Procrastination is deceitful.
- Start with good vegan recipes to change those taste buds of yours.
- There are a lot of vegetable recipes that'll give you a good food experience.
- Have a change of mindset, think positively.
- Be aware of your self-confessions and always say positive, pleasurable things to yourself.
- The positive things are real, but the negative things around you are all a facade. Keep your focus on the positive things of life.
- Have a reprogramming. Reprogram your mind and begin to build your self-confidence.
- Be consistent in what you do – in your diets.

KNOWLEDGE TEST

1. As you begin this plant-based diet and lifestyle, you will need to make several changes. And you need to make them starting now. Do not fall victim to procrastination. Resolve to start making the required changes TODAY, and not tomorrow. The most important day you'll ever experience is TODAY. So, make TODAY the best, most productive and healthiest day, even when circumstances tell you otherwise. That's the only key to success as you begin this plant-based lifestyle. You can start by making your next meal (be it breakfast, lunch or dinner) a healthy plant-based one. Is this true or false? (Check one):
True [   ]
False [   ]

2. You should stay focused on the changes you're making and don't look at what's been taken away from you, because in reality there's really nothing being taken. Focus on training your taste buds to love eating plant-based meals. Eventually you'll get used to it. Is this true or false? (Check one):
True [   ]
False [   ]

3. You can use your mind to get the things you want, to achieve your goals. The mind influences all of our actions. Indeed, the mind is a veritable tool that can cause tremendous changes in your life and environment. What you think is what you get. So, as you begin this plant-based diet and lifestyle, you need to harness the creative power of your mind, the power of your mind to create your circumstances. To succeed, you need to begin to think that you can successfully change your life and your health. You need to begin to think like a healthy, health-conscious, environmentally-conscious, plant-based eating, successful person starting today! Is this true or false? (Check one):
True [ ]
False [ ]

4. When you become a vegan, in the first month, the fact that you now eat like a vegan will prevent the killing of 33 animals and the use of 33,000 gallons of water (for producing food for animals). It will also prevent the destruction of up to 900 square feet of forest and the creation of 600 pounds of carbon dioxide. It will also prevent the diversion of 1,200 pounds of grain for animal food, instead of directing such food to communities that are threatened by hunger. Is this true or false? (Check one):
True [ ]
False [ ]

ACTION STEPS

1. Procrastination is deceitful and can make you put off for tomorrow, that which you can do today. If not carefully checked, it can derail your commendable efforts to change to a plant-based diet and lifestyle. Write down how you plan to defeat procrastination so that you can start embarking on your intended changes TODAY, not tomorrow.

a. _____

b. _____

c. _____

d. _____

2. As you start your plant-based diet and lifestyle, you should focus on training your taste buds to love eating plant-based meals (eventually they'll get used to it). Write down how you plan to achieve this goal. Identify any difficulties and articulate how you will deal with those difficulties.

a. _____

b. _____

c. _____

d. _____

3. Also, as you begin this plant-based diet and lifestyle, you need to harness the power of your mind to create your circumstances. You need to begin to think positively, that is, that you can successfully change your life and your health. You need to reprogram your mind and begin to build your self-confidence and begin to think like a healthy, health-conscious, environmentally-conscious, plant-based eating, successful person. Write down how you plan to achieve this goal. Identify specific mind-training exercises and self-talk/affirmation exercises that you will undertake for this purpose.

a. _____

b. _____

c. _____

d. _____

4. To sustain and maintain your new plant-based diet and lifestyle, consistency is crucial. Write down how you plan to be consistent in this new initiative.

a. _____

b. _____

c. _____

d. _____

CHECKLIST

[ ] Resolve to make my desired changes TODAY, not tomorrow. Do not give in to procrastination.

[ ] Stay focused on my desired changes. 100% focus.

[ ] Train and retrain my taste buds to love eating plant-based meals. Basically, stay on plant-based foods.

[ ] Use the power of my mind to succeed with this plant-based diet and lifestyle program.

[ ] Undertake mind-training exercises and self-talk/affirmation exercises to help me reprogram my mind to help me succeed on this plant-based diet and lifestyle program.

[ ] Be consistent in my determination and purpose. I must succeed in this program and consistency is crucial.

[ ] Retain a good instructor/coach to help me defeat procrastination, stay focused on my desired changes, and remain consistent.

[ ] Surround myself with like-minded persons who will encourage me and help me defeat procrastination, stay focused on my desired changes, and remain consistent.

LAW 15: PERFECTION CAN BE THE ENEMY OF PROGRESS

LESSONS

- Reality isn't based on perfection.
- Concentrate on making progress, not on perfection.
- Being a perfectionist can lead to numerous health problems like anxiety, eating disorders and depression.
- Track your progress and bask in your breakthroughs and accomplishments, that's one of the best feelings ever.

KNOWLEDGE CHECK

1. Man is not perfect. And neither is human society or technology perfect. Real life is not perfect. Perfection is illusory. It is a false attribute. You can never attain perfection. Dietary and lifestyle perfection is nonexistent. If what you want is dietary/lifestyle perfection, then prepare yourself for failure and disappointment. Perfectionism is actually dangerous. It turns you into an enemy of yourself, turns your mind against you, as you wallow in self-criticism. What you want is steady progress towards your goal, not perfection. Is this true or false? (Check one):
True [ ]
False [ ]

2. Sometimes the value of a goal is not necessarily in reaching it (perfectly) but in journeying towards the goal, that is, in making progress towards it. Is this true or false? (Check one):
True [ ]
False [ ]

3. Perfectionism is linked to numerous health issues, including depression, anxiety and eating disorders. Is this true or false? (Check one):
True [ ]
False [ ]

4. Scientific research has also confirmed that the risk of death is significantly higher among perfectionist than among those who do not have that personality trait. Is this true or false? (Check one):
True [ ]
False [ ]

5. Begin with one dietary change (e.g. meatless lunches), and then build on that and make further progress. Progress can be very incremental. Is this true or false? (Check one):
True [ ]
False [ ]

6. Keeping track of your progress is also important. Set particular dietary or lifestyle goals and monitor your progress as you journey towards that goal. Use built-in progress-markers for your goals (that is short term objectives for your medium-term or long-term goals. Remember the point is not necessarily about the destination. It is actually about the journey (the progress towards the destination). Is this true or false? (Check one):
True [ ]
False [ ]

ACTION STEPS

1. Dietary or lifestyle perfectionism is dangerous, as perfection is merely illusory. Perfectionism sets you up for failure and turns you into an enemy of yourself, turns your mind against you, as you wallow in self-criticism. In as much as you desire to adopt a plant-based diet and lifestyle, write down how you plan to protect yourself from the lure of perfectionism.

a. _____

b. _____

c. _____

d. _____

2. *"Sometimes the value of a goal is not necessarily in reaching it (perfectly) but in journeying towards the goal, that is, in making progress towards it"*. Write

down what you think this statement means and explain how it relates to your desired plant-based diet and lifestyle change.

a. _____

b. _____

c. _____

d. _____

3. *"Start modestly and build on humble achievements to make further progress. Progress can be very incremental"*. Write down what you think this statement means and explain how it relates to your desired plant-based diet and lifestyle change.

a. _____

b. _____

c. _____

d. _____

4. Keeping track of your progress is important. Write down how you plan to monitor, evaluate and keep track of your progress as you embark on this plant-based diet and lifestyle program.

a. _____

b. _____

c. _____

d. _____

CHECKLIST

[ ] I am not perfect. But I'll put in great effort and I will make steady progress towards my new diet and lifestyle goals.

[ ] Remember that perfectionism is linked to numerous health issues, including depression, anxiety, eating disorders and even a higher risk of death. Perfectionism is not good for me.

[ ] Begin with a modest change and then build on that and make further progress. Remember, progress is incremental.

[ ] For my dietary and lifestyle goals, set short-term objectives, and medium-term and long-term goals. Use my short-term objectives to work steadily towards my medium-term and long-term dietary and lifestyle goals.

[ ] Keep track of my efforts and activities and constantly monitor and periodically evaluate my progress towards my goals.

LAW 16: LISTEN TO YOUR BODY

LESSONS

- No one can ever know your body better than you do.
- Symptoms are signals or alarms which signify that something isn't right.
- Our bodies are honest tools, they send us alarms; how you respond to these alarms determines their influence over subsequent occurrences.
- Pay attention to your body and answer it when it calls.
- Each individual carries his or her own doctor inside.

KNOWLEDGE CHECK

1. Conventional medicine sometimes fails. And diet and lifestyle changes sometimes hold the answers. For example, physicians typically prescribe drugs as the first line of treatment for hypertension, but the statistics are that for 80% of patients with mild to moderate blood pressure, drugs are not necessarily option for treatment. Is this true or false? (Check one):
True [   ]
False [   ]

2. There is another alternative treatment for hypertension and that is *eating more plants and getting more exercise*. In fact, the Dietary Approaches to Stop Hypertension (DASH) research findings have confirmed that a low-fat diet (includes vegetables, fruits, vegetables, and low-saturated-fat foods) can equally lower blood pressure as well as drugs. Is this true or false? (Check one):
True [   ]
False [   ]

3. A 100%, whole-foods, plant-based diet along with daily moderate exercises, can drop blood pressure dramatically and even normalize it eventually. Is this true or false? (Check one):
True [   ]
False [   ]

4. Symptoms of medical problems are only signs or warning signals. Symptoms have an underlying cause which must be addressed in order to treat the problem. If

you focus on treating the symptoms without addressing the underlying cause, then the medical issue is likely to remain. Unfortunately, conventional medicine tends to focus on symptoms without probing deeper to understand and address the underlying cause. Is this true or false? (Check one):
True [ ]
False [ ]

5. For effective interventions, however (whether by conventional medicine or by diet and lifestyle changes) you need to know early enough, when something goes wrong with your body. And you can do this by listening to your body. Your body will usually tell you everything. And you know your body more than anyone else. So, you need to listen to your body. And when it speaks to you do not ignore what it says. Is this true or false? (Check one):
True [ ]
False [ ]

6. The human body naturally comes with an in-built alarm system to warn us of any possible damage to our body before it gets worse. When you receive this warning from your body, you can either ignore the warning or respond to it. Do not ignore the warnings from your body. Respond appropriately. Indeed, you are better off if you deal with the issues right away. By understanding what's happening inside you and responding appropriately, you can achieve better health. Is this true or false? (Check one):
True [ ]
False [ ]

7. Be proactive about your health. Do not put off that medical checkup again. Avoid procrastination as any delay may result in severe complications, either at the moment or sometime in the future. You are better off acknowledging and responding immediately to your body's messages and warnings. That is the way to better health and longevity. Is this true or false? (Check one):
True [ ]
False [ ]

8. The bottom line is that you need to know the state of your health at any given time. So that makes regular checkups and screening necessary. Remember that the chances of successfully treating a disease are greater if the disease is detected early. Is this true or false? (Check one):
True [ ]
False [ ]

ACTION STEPS

1. Other than conventional medicine, there is another alternative treatment for hypertension. Describe that alternative treatment. In addition, describe the findings of the DASH study as it relates to diet, blood pressure and conventional drugs.

   a. _____

   b. _____

   c. _____

   d. _____

2. A 100%, whole-foods, plant-based diet along with daily moderate exercises, can drop blood pressure dramatically and even normalize it eventually. But is high blood pressure the only condition that this type of approach can treat? Write down other diseases and conditions that can be treated via the treatment approach that includes 100%, whole-foods, plant-based diet along with daily moderate exercises:

   a. _____

   b. _____

   c. _____

   d. _____

3. Symptoms of medical problems are only signs or warning signals. Symptoms have an underlying cause which must be addressed in order to treat the problem. Write down all the symptoms that you have.

   a. _____

   b. _____

   c. _____

   d. _____

4. Write down your plan of how you intend to know early enough, when something goes wrong with your body. Explain whether your plan includes any role for (i)

listening to your body, (ii) going for regular medical checkups, and (iii) going for medical screenings.

a. _____

b. _____

c. _____

d. _____

5. The human body naturally comes with an in-built alarm system to warn us of any possible damage to our body before it gets worse. Write down your plan of how and when you intend to react to any such warnings/signals from your body.

a. _____

b. _____

c. _____

d. _____

CHECKLIST

[ ] Remain consistent with my whole foods, plant-based eating and exercising. Don't give up.

[ ] With medical issues, focus on understanding and addressing the underlying causes instead of seeking only to treat the symptoms.

[ ] Always listen to my body.

[ ] Do not ignore what my body says to me. Respond immediately and appropriately to the warnings that my body gives me.

[ ] Be proactive about my health. Do not put off medical checkups again.

[ ] Avoid procrastination generally, and especially when it comes to my health.

[ ] Ensure that I know the state of my health at any given time.

[ ] Go for regular medical checkups and screenings.

LAW 17: FOCUS ON WHAT YOU CAN EAT, NOT WHAT YOU CAN'T

LESSONS

- Keep your attention on nutrition first; then choose from among the plant-based foods you enjoy.
- Don't force yourself on foods you don't like even if they are nutritious. There are various food alternatives available that are equally nutritious.
- You will need some time to get used to the new flavors of your new food choices.
- Have fun varying your foods (meal variety). Feel free to experiment with food possibilities, but ensure you remain within the stated Greenprint guidelines.

KNOWLEDGE CHECK

1. When following a plant-based diet, your choice of the foods you eat should be based on the nutritional contents of the food. Is this true or false? (Check one):
True [   ]
False [   ]

2. When following a plant-based diet, you should feel very deprived because of the various unhealthy (but perhaps sweet-tasting) foods you cannot eat. You should also be very upset because you will no longer have to stock unhealthy, processed foods in your kitchen. Is this true or false? (Check one):
True [   ]
False [   ]

3. When following a plant-based diet, you should eat only foods that you enjoy and that can give you a whole lot of good nutrients. Is this true or false? (Check one):
True [   ]
False [   ]

4. When following a plant-based diet, you should avoid processed foods, even if they're plant-based. Is this true or false? (Check one):
True [   ]
False [   ]

5. When foods are processed, a lot of fiber and other minute nutrients are extracted, so that it would be easier and quicker to consume such foods and ask for more. Is this true or false? (Check one):
True [ ]
False [ ]

6. When following a plant-based diet, you should stock your kitchen fully with the following delicious processed foods: (i) added or additive sugar, (ii) processed white flour, (iii) artificial sweeteners, (iv) processed (and unprocessed) dairy products, (v) and meat. Is this true or false? (Check one):
True [ ]
False [ ]

7. When following a plant-based diet, you should stop bothering yourself about what you shouldn't eat, and instead focus on eating the foods you enjoy that will *also* give you good health. Always have this kind of mutual relationship with your food. Is this true or false? (Check one):
True [ ]
False [ ]

8. The more you eat healthy, plant-based foods, the more your taste buds will become trained to love plant-based foods and the more you will begin to enjoy plant-based foods. Is this true or false? (Check one):
True [ ]
False [ ]

9. You should be optimistic, especially with your new plant-based diet and lifestyle habits. Optimism is very good for your health. Is this true or false? (Check one):
True [ ]
False [ ]

10. Scientific research has found that optimistic people have a lower risk of having cardiovascular illnesses as compared to pessimistic people. Is this true or false? (Check one):
True [ ]
False [ ]

ACTION STEPS

1. When following a plant-based diet, your choice of the foods you eat should be based on the nutritional contents of the food. Write down how you plan to ensure that your food choices are nutritious. Give examples.

a. _____

b. _____

c. _____

d. _____

2. When following a plant-based diet, you may occasionally feel deprived and upset because of the various unhealthy foods you can no longer eat or stock in your kitchen. Write down how you plan to cope with and survive those moments without falling to temptation. Specify how you intend to acquire the resources that can help you to get through those moments.

a. _____

b. _____

c. _____

d. _____

3. When following a plant-based diet, you should avoid processed foods, even if they're plant-based. So, take an inventory of the food items in your home and write a list of all the processed foods currently stocked in your home. Also write a sub-list of those food items among them that are plant-based processed foods.

a. _____

b. _____

c. _____

d. _____

4. Discard all the processed food items that are currently stocked in your home. Then write down here a list of the processed food items you have discarded. Indicate whether or not you will be re-stocking your home with these processed food items any time in future.

a. _____

b. _____

c. _____

d. _____

5. It is important to train your taste buds to adjust to plant-based eating. Write down how you plan to train your taste buds so that they can get used to and love plant-based foods, so that ultimately you will truly begin to enjoy plant-based foods?

a. _____

b. _____

c. _____

d. _____

6. As you follow a plant-based diet, it is crucial that you remain optimistic about yourself, about your new plant-based diet and lifestyle and about your chances of success. Write down how you plan to maintain and sustain your optimism as you move forward. Specify the resources that can help you achieve this objective and specify how you intend to acquire those resources.

a. _____

b. _____

c. _____

d. _____

CHECKLIST

[ ] Base my food choices on whether I enjoy eating a particular food ***in addition*** to whether the food is nutritious.

[ ] Do not feel deprived or upset about the various foods I can no longer eat or stock in my kitchen. Such foods are unhealthy foods anyway and would eventually harm me if I did not cease eating them.

[ ] Avoid processed foods, even if they're plant-based.

[ ] Ensure that none of the under-listed foods are stocked in my kitchen: (i) added or additive sugar, (ii) processed white flour, (iii) artificial sweeteners, (iv) processed (and unprocessed) dairy products, (v) and meat.

[ ] Remember that the healthier I eat, the more my taste buds will become trained to love plant-based foods.

[ ] At all times, remain optimistic about myself, about my plant-based diet and lifestyle and about my chances of success with the Greenprint lifestyle.

LAW 18: PLANTS HAVE ALL THE POWER WE NEED

LESSONS

- To be strong and powerful, we must not eat meat.
- Plant-based diets are an adequate source of protein. Plant-based foods can also help to decrease inflammation in the body.
- Athletes and exercisers can source from plants and vegan proteins, certain essential amino acids that the body needs for muscle building and repair.
- Mind how much Vitamin D, Vitamin B12, Zinc, Iron, and Omega-3 fatty acids you are consuming. You can get all these vitamins from plants.
- Athletes can still excel on a plant-based diet. Meat is not necessary for an athlete's diet.
- Even in strength sports (e.g. weight training), an athlete can get enough of the protein he needs from plants.
- So, it is very possible to succeed in the highly intensive world of sports while following a plant-based diet.
- If you follow Greenprint Law No. 18 you'll get enough antioxidants that will protect you from free radicals.

KNOWLEDGE CHECK

1. For a human being to be powerful and strong, that person must eat meat. Is this true or false? (Check one):
True [   ]
False [   ]

2. Some of the biggest and most powerful animals in the world today (e.g., elephants, rhinos, gorillas, buffaloes, etc.) are plant eaters. Is this true or false? (Check one):
True [   ]
False [   ]

3. And some of the fastest, strongest, and most powerful athletes in the world today are also plant eaters. Is this true or false? (Check one):
True [   ]
False [   ]

4. A plant-based diet cannot provide adequate levels of protein to the body and certainly not enough protein to meet the demand of athletes. Is this true or false? (Check one):
True [   ]
False [   ]

5. Plant-based foods do not reduce inflammation in the body, and they do not supply the body with antioxidants that defend the body against free radicals. Is this true or false? (Check one):
True [   ]
False [   ]

6. There are nine essential amino acids that the body needs for muscle growth and repair (but which the body cannot produce by itself). Those nine essential amino acids are: isoleucine, leucine, lysine, methionine and cysteine, phenylalanine and tyrosine, threonine, tryptophan, valine, and histidine. Athletes need these essential amino acids more, because of regular muscular exertion. And athletes can get **all** those essential amino acids from plants proteins such as buckwheat, quinoa, chia seed, and hempseed. Is this true or false? (Check one):
True [   ]
False [   ]

7. Vitamin D, Vitamin B12, Zinc, Iron and Omega-3 fatty acids that are also very important for athletes are also available from plants such as fruits, vegetables, seeds, nuts, beans and legumes. Is this true or false? (Check one):
True [   ]
False [   ]

8. So, meat is not necessary for an athlete's diet. A plant-based diet can still improve an athlete's cardiovascular health; improve their energy, endurance and muscle growth and repair. It can also reduce recovery time for sore, injured or over-worked muscles (as is typical with athletes). Is this true or false? (Check one):
True [   ]
False [   ]

9. And even with strength sports (e.g. weight training), an athlete can still source all of his/her protein from plants. In short, despite people's misconception, it is, indeed, still very possible to excel in competitive sports while one is strictly on a plant-based diet. Is this true or false? (Check one):
True [   ]
False [   ]

ACTION STEPS

1. Do some research, find out and write down here, the names of some persons who are physical big, strong and powerful, but who are mostly plant eaters (vegetarians or vegans or 100% plant-based eaters).

a. _____

b. _____

c. _____

d. _____

2. Do some research, find out and write down here, the names of some of the well-known and accomplished athletes in competitive sports who are mostly plant eaters (vegetarians or vegans or 100% plant-based eaters).

a. _____

b. _____

c. _____

d. _____

3. A plant-based diet can provide adequate levels of protein to the body and certainly it can provide enough protein to meet even the demand of professional athletes. Is this true or false? Explain your answer in detail.

a. _____

b. _____

c. _____

d. _____

CHECKLIST

[ ] Avoid meat and all animal-based food products. I do not need to eat meat to be physically fit, big, fast, powerful, strong or athletic.

[　] Keep on following a plant-based diet. Never give up!

[　] Always remember that a plant-based diet can provide me with more than adequate levels of protein; reduce inflammation in my body; supply my body with antioxidants that defend my body against free radicals; supply my body with essential amino acids that my body needs for muscle growth and repair; supply my body with Vitamin D, Vitamin B12, Zinc, Iron, and Omega-3 fatty acids; improve my cardiovascular health; improve my energy and endurance; improve the recovery time for my sore, injured or over-worked muscles; reduce my fatigue from over-exertion and improve the overall state of my health. So, I am on the right track by following a plant-based diet.

LAW 19: A BEHAVIOR THAT IS REWARDED WOULD BE REPEATED

LESSONS

- Enjoy yourself in every way as you transcend to plant-based diets.
- Don't give up what you like because you want to try your best to improve on your health, you'll fail.
- If you have pleasure for what you do, whether it's eating a plant-based diet or exercising, your reward can be phenomenal. You would definitely have a better mental clarity.
- Motivate yourself towards your goal. Do not wait for anyone to do it for you.
- Do away with bad habits.
- Prioritize. Set clear goals that you wish to achieve.
- Remain focused on the goal you wish to achieve.
- Find friends and make friends that will assist and support you.

KNOWLEDGE CHECK

1. To be successful with this plant-based diet and lifestyle program, you should not try to force yourself to adjust to the new habits that are required. Instead, you should relax and enjoy the journey, step by step. Is this true or false? (Check one):
True [ ]
False [ ]

2. Success in the plant-based eating and lifestyle program requires that you do the healthy things that make you happy. Simply eat the healthy foods that taste good to you and start from there. That is the winning plan for acquiring the new habit. Is this true or false? (Check one):
True [ ]
False [ ]

3. As you try to settle into the plant-based diet and lifestyle program, if you force yourself to do the things you clearly hate to do; if you try to give up all the foods you love, you'll get absolutely nowhere. Most likely you'd eventually give up and flunk out. Is this true or false? (Check one):
True [ ]
False [ ]

4. To avoid the above from happening, you need to enjoy the process. You need to flow with the change and enjoy the change. You need to find a niche, a place of enjoyment within the plant-based diet and lifestyle program. You need to start from that place of enjoyment and just flow with the program, knowing that it will get better and easier with time. Is this true or false? (Check one):
True [ ]
False [ ]

5. You also need to be optimistic and have a positive view about this diet and lifestyle change. Optimism will make your mind to become clearer and you will begin to see and experience the health benefits of plant-based eating which will encourage you to do more for yourself. Is this true or false? (Check one):
True [ ]
False [ ]

6. You also need to celebrate your successes (no matter how little they may be). By celebrating and rewarding your successes (even if they are small) you'll be motivated to sustain good habits and do away with bad, unwholesome habits. Is this true or false? (Check one):
True [ ]
False [ ]

7. You also need to learn how to manage your difficulties and setbacks effectively. Basically, do not allow them to overwhelm you, or to incapacitate you from engaging in other efforts towards your ultimate goal. Work around them, if need be, until you are able to resolve them. But at all times, certainly keep moving forward towards your goal. Is this true or false? (Check one):
True [ ]
False [ ]

ACTION STEPS

1. To be successful with this plant-based diet and lifestyle program, you should not try to force yourself to adjust to the new habits. Instead, you should relax and enjoy the journey, step by step. **But assuming you are finding it difficult to "relax and enjoy" the process, write down how you plan to resolve this challenge. Identify the resources that you would rely on to resolve this challenge and specify how you intend to acquire and how you intend to utilize those resources.**
   a. _____

b. _____

c. _____

d. _____

2. Success in the plant-based eating and lifestyle program requires that you do the healthy things that make you happy. Simply eat the healthy foods that taste good to you and start from there. **List the healthy foods you like to eat.**

a. _____

b. _____

c. _____

d. _____

3. As you try to settle into the plant-based diet and lifestyle program, if you force yourself to do the things you clearly hate to do; if you try to give up all the foods you love, you'll get absolutely nowhere. **List some assume heathy foods or routines that you dislike and articulate a plan of how you will handle the issue.**

a. _____

b. _____

c. _____

d. _____

4. Explain your place of enjoyment within the plant-based diet and lifestyle program.

a. _____

b. _____

c. _____

d. _____

5. How do you plan to cultivate and maintain your optimism about this Greenprint diet and lifestyle program?

a. _____

b. _____

c. _____

d. _____

CHECKLIST

[ ] Will not force myself to adjust to the Greenprint program or to do the things I hate. Instead will relax and enjoy the journey.

[ ] Do the things that make me happy. Eat the healthy foods that taste good and start from there.

[ ] Will find and own a niche that I enjoy within the Greenprint program.

[ ] Will remain optimistic and positive about myself, and the Greenprint program.

[ ] Will always celebrate my successes, no matter how little they may be.

[ ] Will not dwell too much on my difficulties and setbacks.

LAW 20: YOU CANNOT GIVE WHAT YOU DO NOT HAVE

LESSONS
- Make sure you take care of yourself first, before helping out in urgent matters.
- If you're physically and emotionally down, you can't give anything to other people around you.
- Take out some time and enjoy yourself.
- Give yourself good time to avoid fizzling out.

KNOWLEDGE CHECK

1. Always take care of yourself first. This does not mean you should do it to the extreme and become a narcissist. Take some time to work on your habits. Eat the right things and enjoy a good day at the park or the beach (whichever you choose). This is the key to living in optimal health. Is this true or false? (Check one):
True [ ]
False [ ]

2. You can take real good care of yourself in these ways: get committed to law one "eat more plants"; always drink water.; enjoy something you love doing physically; take time off from social media and all of technology; pamper your body a little bit; always get a good night's sleep; make some time to just have FUN!; and learn how to be emotionally stable and intelligent. Is this true or false? (Check one):
True [ ]
False [ ]

3. If you take care of yourself first, you will notice that you will begin to meet other external responsibilities with increasing ease. Is this true or false? (Check one):
True [ ]
False [ ]

4. If you begin to take care of yourself first, you will have to begin eating only plant-based foods. Plant-based foods will keep you healthy, vibrant and strong and protect your body from terminal diseases. Is this true or false? (Check one):
True [ ]
False [ ]

ACTION STEPS

1. Explain your plan of how you intend to take care of yourself first and how you plan to keep it within acceptable limits to avoid narcissism.

a. _____

b. _____

c. _____

d. _____

2. Write down some of the healthy, safe and blameless ways you can enjoy and take care of yours, that are recommended in the book, The Greenprint.

a. _____

b. _____

c. _____

d. _____

CHECKLIST

[ ] Remember to take care of myself first, but to take care to avoid narcissism.

[ ] Enjoy my life and take care of myself first, in healthy, safe and blameless ways.

[ ] Remember, if I am physically and emotionally down, I can't give anything to or help other people around me. So, again, take care of myself first!

LAW 21: BRING MINDFULNESS TO EATING

LESSONS

- Let your mind be aware of the food you eat in all its ramifications.
- Slow down, don't rush. Slow down and take pleasure while preparing and eating your food.
- Mindful eating also involves minding how your food is prepared; how it is served; the kind of behavior at the dining table and the type of people with whom you eat.
- There is a huge sense of satisfaction in mindful cooking and eating.

KNOWLEDGE CHECK

1. Mindful eating is one of the best ways to reduce your weight. People get overweight or obese because of the way they view and act towards food (being unmindful of the function of food in our body). Mindful eating focuses on what foods we eat and how our bodies feel or react when eating them. It is all about slowing down and enjoying our food and eating experience. Is this true or false? (Check one):
True [ ]
False [ ]

2. Mindful eating also involves minding how your food is prepared; how it is served; the kind of behavior at the dining table; the type of people with whom you eat and even your attitude or stance at the dining table (these are highly important). Is this true or false? (Check one):
True [ ]
False [ ]

3. Make a plant-based recipe for yourself. Add all you wish, to make the experience a unique one to remember. Fix you mind and savor the entire food/eating process (from preparation, to cooking, to dressing and serving). If you want to lose a great deal of weight, make sure to follow this law. Eating mindfully can help you maintain a healthy weight. Is this true or false? (Check one):
True [ ]
False [ ]

4. By bringing mindfulness to eating, you'll be able to increase your thoughtfulness around the preparation and eating of your food. This will translate into a happier you and better health for you, eventually. Is this true or false? (Check one):
True [ ]
False [ ]

ACTION STEPS

1. What is "mindful eating"? What are the benefits of "mindful eating"?
a. _____

b. _____

c. _____

d. _____

2. Describe your plan for henceforth implementing "mindful eating" in your life, and explain why it is important that you do so.
a. _____

b. _____

c. _____

d. _____

CHECKLIST

[ ] Practice "mindful eating", always.

[ ] Take food/eating slow and easy. Do not rush. Be mindful and take pleasure in the entire process.

LAW 22: PRACTICE KAIZEN

LESSONS

- If you think your goals are impossible to achieve, practice Kaizen.
- Kaizen is Japanese and it means, "little improvements count a lot".
- Kaizen can help you to form positive habits.
- Use kaizen for exercising and for plant-based eating. You'll experience tremendous health improvements.

KNOWLEDGE CHECK

1. Kaizen is a Japanese word and it means "good change". When you need to make a transformative change in your life (e.g. in losing weight and forming new or breaking old habits), practice Kaizen. Kaizen encourages a person to watch closely and make little but important changes that will ultimately and cumulatively have a big impact. Kaizen is a great tool that most people can use to enhance their physical fitness and dietary habits. Is this true or false? (Check one):
True [ ]
False [ ]

2. As you begin the process of using Kaizen (perhaps for your daily workout or for a change to plant-based diets), you'll have to be patient, because your brain is reprogramming and it takes some time for new mental pathways and connections to be created in your brain. Is this true or false? (Check one):
True [ ]
False [ ]

3. With Kaizen, when you choose an action and continuously repeat it over the course of some days, weeks or even months (basically when you STAY ON IT), eventually the desired change will come. Is this true or false? (Check one):
True [ ]
False [ ]

4. By practicing Kaizen, you simply become patient. Patience is the key to living a healthy and strong lifestyle. Don't be anxious, be patient and work on your goals a bit at a time, step-by-step, little-by-little, and you will see yourself improving every day. Is this true or false? (Check one):
True [ ]
False [ ]

ACTION STEPS

1. Articulate your plan for henceforth practicing Kaizen in your life, and explain why it is important that you do so.

   a. _____

   b. _____

   c. _____

   d. _____

2. Explain the importance of "patience" to the practice of Kaizen.

   a. _____

   b. _____

   c. _____

   d. _____

CHECKLIST

[ ] Practice Kaizen. It can help me to form positive habits.

[ ] Use Kaizen for my exercising and plant-based eating goals.

PART 2: LIVING THE GREENPRINT LAWS: THE THREE TRANSITIONAL TIERS

CHECKLIST FOR LIVING THE GREEN PRINT LAWS

[ ] Apply the Greenprint laws via the three transitional tiers.

[ ] Overall, apply the Kaizen approach so you can make the desired change gradually.

[ ] In Tier 1: (the gradual shift), begin eating one plant-based meal a day for a maximum of eleven days.

[ ] In Tier 2: (the ramp up): begin eating eat two plant-based meals for eleven days.

[ ] In Tier 3: (the full on): now, go wholly plant-based. Now you are in full Vegan mode.

TIER 1: THE GRADUAL SHIFT

CHECKLIST FOR TIER 1: THE GRADUAL SHIFT

[   ] Tier 1 is all about eating one plant-based meal for eleven days.

[   ] The plant-based meal could be either your breakfast
, lunch or dinner

[   ] Alternatively, you can take your one-a-day plant-based meals in succession (that is, take one plant-based meal as breakfast in the first day; make it your lunch in the following day; and make it dinner the next day, and so on).

[   ] Choose only meals you find quite palatable and enjoy.

[   ] While you're on Tier 1 begin to discard any of these animal-based food products: cheese, eggs, honey, fish and shell fish, chicken, dairy products, beef, pork, lamb or all red meat.

[   ] During this eleven-day Tier 1 period, learn as much as you can about: plant-based living, the benefits of plant-based living; how to nourish your body; and the costs to you and society of the production of animal-based food products.

[   ] During this eleven-day Tier 1 period, always keep your Kaizen goals in mind. And the goals are: the consumption of one plant-based meal per day for 11 days plus the elimination of 1 or 2 animal-based food products from your diet.

TIER 2: THE RAMP UP

CHECKLIST FOR TIER 2: THE RAMP UP

[   ] In Tier 2, for the next eleven days, commit yourself to eating two plant-based meals daily.

[   ] This could be breakfast and lunch or lunch and dinner. Plan whatever combination of meal that works for you.

[   ] Tier 2 is primarily about reducing your consumption of animal-based foods, while increasing your consumption of plant-based foods.

[   ] Cut out more animal-based foods from your diet.

[   ] Stay motivated. You can do this! At this time, it is important for you to always review the reasons for and benefits of a plant-based diet and the consequences of consuming animal-based products (both in terms of the impact on health, and on the environment).

[   ] If you do this constantly it will keep you motivated and you won't stray from the plant-based lifestyle progress that you are making. Once this sinks in, there's no stopping you now!

TIER 3: THE FULL-ON

CHECKLIST FOR TIER 3: THE FULL-ON

[   ] In Tier 3, for the next forty-four day period, begin to eat three plant-based meals and snacks every day, in other words, you'll have to go 100% plant-based!

[   ] At this stage, remove any and all traces of animal-based food products from all of your meals.

[   ] Do not worry about animal-sourced proteins. Replace them with plant-based proteins.

[   ] Pay absolute attention to products or food information/labels and avoid foods that contain gelatin or rennet and other animal products like eggs and dairy products.

[   ] Look for and try out some good vegan restaurants. Remember that there are some continental or ethnic restaurants, Chinese, Indian, Japanese, Mediterranean, and Mexican restaurants that serve a variety of plant-based foods. Try them all! Have fun!

[   ] **HAVE FUN!** (the boldened upper case is on purpose). Have fun! Have a ball and enjoy yourself!

CONCLUSION: BE THE GREENPRINT

It's good to start the GREENPRINT with the intention of making good improvements to your health and well-being. But the best motivation for the program is to improve the planets health. Living the Greenprint will help to heal our planet.

And as you journey in the program, take note of any changes you notice in your health/body (while on the program). Take note of things like, endurance, strength, recovery, increased energy weight loss, sex drive, sleep quality and overall energy. Take this evaluation bit by bit, by applying the 22nd law - the Kaizen method.

Be mindful of your overall GREENPRINT and of the impact that your food decisions and lifestyle have on the earth. You can be the change you desire. We've all heard about climate change and how the earth is declining in productivity. There is a direct connection between our food choices and the increase in greenhouse gases, global warming and human activity.

You can help in sustaining and saving the planet by buying only locally grown foods. This helps to save energy and also to increase health. Go to a farm market, instead of the supermarket to purchase your food products. Use public transportation instead of driving your car. Grow a garden of vegetables of your choice. Plant trees. Compost, recycle and avoid buying so many manufactured or packaged products. You can make a huge difference in the world.

Start today and improve your world!

APPENDIX A: CERTIFICATE OF COMMITMENT

CERTIFICATE OF COMMITMENT

I, _____,

HEREBY COMMIT MYSELF TO LIVING THE GREENPRINT AND TO FOLLOWING ALL THE GREENPRINT GUIDELINES AS CONTAINED IN THE BOOK, *THE GREENPRINT*, BY MARC BORGES.

SIGNATURE: _____

DATE: _____

WITNESS: _____

APPENDIX B: THE MASTER CHECKLIST

This is a master checklist of all the action items and important points in the book. Review this master checklist every day and ensure that your thoughts and activities are in line with its prescriptions. Some items on the list are repeated on purpose. Consider that as an indication of their extra importance and just get to working and living this master checklist. It's pleasantly challenging and it's fun. So, make sure you have a lot of fun while going at it! You can do it! It's a lot of fun! Let's go!

LAW 1: EAT MORE PLANTS AND EAT LESS OF EVERYTHING ELSE

[ ] Sign the Commitment Certificate (Appendix A), thereby committing myself to eating only a 100% plant-based diet and following all Greenprint guidelines.

[ ] Avoid animal-based food products including beef, pork, poultry, mutton, fish, milk, cheese, butter, mayonnaise eggs and honey etc.

[ ] Eat enough plants and vegetables every day to meet my daily protein requirement.

[ ] Eat enough plants and vegetables every day to meet my daily fiber requirement.

[ ] Eat enough plants and vegetables every day to meet my daily requirement for other nutrients, vitamins and minerals.

[ ] Include beans and legumes in my diet.

[ ] Include nuts and seeds in my diet.

[ ] Include whole grains in my diet.

[ ] Include plant fats in my diet.

[ ] Eat a lot of green vegetables every day.

[　] Eat a lot of colorful vegetables every day.

LAW 2: NOBODY EVER PLANS TO FAIL- PEOPLE JUST FAIL TO PLAN
[　] Plan my switch to plant-based eating.

[　] Accept that I am 100% responsible for the current state of my health and weight through the diet and lifestyle choices I made in the past.

[　] Determine my nutritional needs.

[　] Plan how plant-based diet can meet my nutritional needs

[　] Plan my meals around a variety of high-quality, nutrient-rich foods, such as whole grains, beans, legumes, vegetables, fruits, nuts, and seeds.

[　] Ensure that healthy, plant-based food is always conveniently available and accessible around me.

[　] Ensure that my daily iron requirements are met via my plant-based diet.

[　] Ensure that my daily Vitamin B-12 requirements are met via my plant-based diet.

[　] Ensure that my daily Omega-3 fatty acids requirements are met via my plant-based diet.

[　] Ensure that my daily Vitamin D requirements are met via my plant-based diet.

[　] Ensure that my daily Calcium requirements are met via my plant-based diet.

[　] Ensure that my daily Protein requirements are met via my plant-based diet.

[　] Ensure that my daily Zinc requirements are met via my plant-based diet.

LAW 3: EAT MORE, WEIGH LESS
[　] Engage in daily mind-training exercises so I can train my mind and improve my mental discipline.

[　] Engage in physical training exercises at least four days every week.

[　] Retain a good instructor to guide me on my way to fitness, weight loss and healthy living.

[ ] Surround myself with like-minded persons who will encourage me and assist me on my journey to fitness, weight loss and healthy living.

[ ] Eat only simple, clean, whole plant-based foods. Do not eat over-processed foods.

[ ] Ensure that I get a good dose of fiber, daily, through eating a plant-based diet.

[ ] Change how I think of myself and the food that I eat. Use food to achieve fitness, weight loss and healthy living, and to prevent and beat disease.

LAW 4: WATER IS LIFE FUEL
[ ] FOR A MAN: drink at least thirteen 8-ounce cups of water, daily. FOR A WOMAN: drink at least nine 8-ounce cups of water, daily.

[ ] Eat plenty of fruits and vegetables. Succulent fruits, particularly, contain a large percentage of water.

[ ] Eat at least five servings of fruits and vegetables daily. This can supply my body with 20% of my daily water requirement.

[ ] Conduct the Body-Water-Level Self-Test upon myself regularly, in order to detect and avoid dehydration.

LAW 5: PROTECT YOUR HEART
[ ] Discard all my lifestyle and diet habits which can negatively affect my heart.

[ ] Abstain from eating junk food and meat.

[ ] Eat a strictly 100% plant-based diet, daily.

[ ] Eat four or five servings of fruits and vegetables daily.

[ ] Exercise at least four days per week.

LAW 6: TAKE CARE OF YOUR MIND
[ ] Stay committed to a strictly 100% plant-based diet. Never give up!

[ ] Avoid foods that contain saturated fats.

[ ] Avoid eating meat.

[ ] Eat plant-based foods that are high in polyphenols.

LAW 7: FAST FOR HEALTH AND LONGETIVITY
[ ] Include intermittent fasting in my new lifestyle and dietary change program.

[ ] Get adequate sleep every day. Sleeping is a kind of intermittent fasting which is good for me in many ways. An adult needs between 7 to 9 hours of sleep every night.

LAW 8: THINK ABOUT THE EARTH BEFORE YOU EAT
[ ] Make lifestyle and diet choices that positively impact both my health and the environment.

[ ] Cultivate important and sustainable food habits that can translate into huge differences.

[ ] Become a locavore. Buy and eat only locally grown foods.

[ ] Plan my weekly menus and buy only as much food or produce as I will need for the short term. Do not hoard items or buy in too much bulk because that often leads to waste.

[ ] Choose whole foods over packaged or processed foods.

[ ] Think about the earth before I eat. Doing so will make me more environment-friendly. It will also motivate me to leave the smallest carbon foot-print.

LAW 9: LOVE FOOD THAT LOVES YOU BACK
[ ] Search for and eat only foods that love me. These are the nutrient-rich, healthy, plant-based foods that will improve my health and enhance my longevity.

[ ] Avoid processed foods, sweet foods, and junk food. These are foods that hate me and wish me ill.

[ ] Train my taste buds to love plant-based foods. It's easy. My taste buds can adjust to plant-based foods in only as little as 2 weeks.

[ ] Train my kids not to reject healthy foods. Consistently offer them plant-based foods. Be persistent. With time they'll get used to it.

LAW 10: MOVEMENT BEGETS MOVEMENT
[ ] Do something physical every day, like walking or jogging, etc. A sedentary lifestyle is dangerous.

[ ] Include exercising in my daily routine. Make exercising a habit. Exercise daily.

[ ] Motivation is essential! Maintain my motivation and momentum in my exercise habit. Stick to it! Do not give up! It gets easier with time.

[ ] Engage in weight training and resistance exercises to gain and maintain strength and to help prevent muscular atrophy (wasting away of the muscles), and to lower the risk of developing osteoarthritis or osteoporosis.

LAW 11: TRASH MUST BE TAKEN OUT
[ ] Be more cautious about processed and animal-based foods. They introduce a higher percentage of toxins into our body.

[ ] Drinking water is also another means of achieving detoxification. A glass of water can flush out a mass of toxins through sweat and urine.

[ ] Eat plant-based foods to strengthen the body's detoxification system.

[ ] Consume antioxidant-rich foods to protect yourself against tissue damage which may result from free radicals in the body.

LAW 12: THE WORLD DOESN'T NEED US TO SURVIVE – WE NEED THE WORLD TO SURVIVE
[ ] Remind at least one person each day that plant-based diets are better for the planet than animal-based diets.

[ ] Remind at least one person each day that animal farming is inflicting damage on the earth on a large scale.

[ ] Remember that physiologically the human body (including mine) was made to eat vegetables and fruits, not animals.

[ ] Do not to underestimate the power of the impact of my choices and habits upon the environment. So, in my daily choices of how I transport myself, what I eat, what kind of clothes I buy, etc., I will be wise and consider my health and the heath of the environment. Indeed, the daily choices I make and habits I practice can ultimately change the entire food system and stabilize the world.

[ ] Eat only plant-based foods. The foods we choose to eat affect not only us but also the environment and our planet both positively and negatively.

[ ] Avoid eating hamburgers, meat generally and other processed animal-based food products.

[ ] Also avoid eating the typical meat-heavy American diet. Eat only plant-based foods.

[ ] Take other measures on my own initiative to protect the environment, reduce my carbon footprint and protect my health.

[ ] Influence my family members and those close to me to eat only plant-based foods; to avoid eating hamburgers, meat generally and other processed animal-based food products; to avoid eating the typical meat-heavy American diet; and to take other measures on their own initiative to protect the environment, reduce their carbon footprint and protect their health.

LAW 13: CHANGE STARTS WITH YOU
[ ] I understand that the change the planet needs starts with me.

[ ] Examine my habits, choices and lifestyle on a daily basis to determine where I have to make a change.

[ ] Make good food choices every day. Basically, eat only plant-based foods.

[ ] Scale back on my food and produce budget and buy only things that are necessary and in limited quantity

[ ] Conduct a daily examination to ensure that the way I cook, the way I store my food and the way I dispose of my waste, etc., are all environmentally friendly.

[ ] Begin to use energy-efficient technologies immediately.

[ ] Begin to set my appliances appropriately so that they can use minimal power. Also turn off my appliances that are not in use so I can save on power. Begin this immediately.

[ ] Prepare my own meals. Avoid buying fast food. This is beneficial for my health.

[ ] Do not eat meat, animal-based food products and processed foods.

[ ] Use my money, my purchasing power to better the planet. Do not patronize companies and products that maintain unsustainable and environmentally unfriendly practices.

[ ] Always think of new and creative ways to reduce my environmental footprint.

[ ] Remind at least one person each day that the change our planet needs starts with each of us, personally.

LAW 14: THE BEST STARTING POINT IS TODAY
[ ] Resolve to make my desired changes TODAY, not tomorrow. Do not give in to procrastination.

[ ] Stay focused on my desired changes. 100% focus.

[ ] Train and retrain my taste buds to love eating plant-based meals. Basically, stay on plant-based foods.

[ ] Use the power of my mind to succeed with this plant-based diet and lifestyle program.

[ ] Undertake mind-training exercises and self-talk/affirmation exercises to help me reprogram my mind to help me succeed on this plant-based diet and lifestyle program.

[ ] Be consistent in my determination and purpose. I must succeed in this program and consistency is crucial.

[ ] Retain a good instructor/coach to help me defeat procrastination, stay focused on my desired changes, and remain consistent.

[ ] Surround myself with like-minded persons who will encourage me and help me defeat procrastination, stay focused on my desired changes, and remain consistent.

LAW 15: PERFECTION CAN BE THE ENEMY OF PROGRESS
[ ] I am not perfect. But I'll put in great effort and I will make steady progress towards my new diet and lifestyle goals.

[ ] Remember that perfectionism is linked to numerous health issues, including depression, anxiety, eating disorders and even a higher risk of death. Perfectionism is not good for me.

[ ] Begin with a modest change and then build on that and make further progress. Remember, progress is incremental.

[ ] For my dietary and lifestyle goals, set short-term objectives, and medium-term and long-term goals. Use my short-term objectives to work steadily towards my medium-term and long-term dietary and lifestyle goals.

[ ] Keep track of my efforts and activities and constantly monitor and periodically evaluate my progress towards my goals.

LAW 16: LISTEN TO YOUR BODY

[ ] Remain consistent with my whole foods, plant-based eating and exercising. Don't give up.

[ ] With medical issues, focus on understanding and addressing the underlying causes instead of seeking only to treat the symptoms.

[ ] Always listen to my body.

[ ] Do not ignore what my body says to me. Respond immediately and appropriately to the warnings that my body gives me.

[ ] Be proactive about my health. Do not put off medical checkups again.

[ ] Avoid procrastination generally, and especially when it comes to my health.

[ ] Ensure that I know the state of my health at any given time.

[ ] Go for regular medical checkups and screenings.

LAW 17: FOCUS ON WHAT YOU CAN EAT, NOT WHAT YOU CAN'T

[ ] Base my food choices on whether I enjoy eating a particular food **in addition** to whether the food is nutritious.

[ ] Do not feel deprived or upset about the various foods I can no longer eat or stock in my kitchen. Such foods are unhealthy foods anyway and would eventually harm me if I did not cease eating them.

[ ] Avoid processed foods, even if they're plant-based.

[ ] Ensure that none of the under-listed foods are stocked in my kitchen: (i) added or additive sugar, (ii) processed white flour, (iii) artificial sweeteners, (iv) processed (and unprocessed) dairy products, (v) and meat.

[ ] Remember that the healthier I eat, the more my taste buds will become trained to love plant-based foods.

[ ] At all times, remain optimistic about myself, about my plant-based diet and lifestyle and about my chances of success with the Greenprint lifestyle.

LAW 18: PLANTS HAVE ALL THE POWER WE NEED
[ ] Avoid meat and all animal-based food products. I do not need to eat meat to be physically fit, big, fast, powerful, strong or athletic.

[ ] Keep on following a plant-based diet. Never give up!

[ ] Always remember that a plant-based diet can provide me with more than adequate levels of protein; reduce inflammation in my body; supply my body with antioxidants that defend my body against free radicals; supply my body with essential amino acids that my body needs for muscle growth and repair; supply my body with Vitamin D, Vitamin B12, Zinc, Iron, and Omega-3 fatty acids; improve my cardiovascular health; improve my energy and endurance; improve the recovery time for my sore, injured or over-worked muscles; reduce my fatigue from over-exertion and improve the overall state of my health. So, I am on the right track by following a plant-based diet.

LAW 19: A BEHAVIOR THAT IS REWARDED WOULD BE REPEATED
[ ] Will not force myself to adjust to the Greenprint program or to do the things I hate. Instead will relax and enjoy the journey.

[ ] Do the things that make me happy. Eat the healthy foods that taste good and start from there.

[ ] Will find and own a niche that I enjoy within the Greenprint program.

[ ] Will remain optimistic and positive about myself, and the Greenprint program.

[ ] Will always celebrate my successes, no matter how little they may be.

[ ] Will not dwell too much on my difficulties and setbacks.

LAW 20: YOU CANNOT GIVE WHAT YOU DO NOT HAVE
[ ] Remember to take care of myself first, but to take care to avoid narcissism.

[ ] Enjoy my life and take care of myself first, in healthy, safe and blameless ways.

[ ] Remember, if I am physically and emotionally down, I can't give anything to or help other people around me. So, again, take care of myself first!

LAW 21: BRING MINDFULNESS TO EATING
[ ] Practice "mindful eating", always.

[ ] Take food/eating slow and easy. Do not rush. Be mindful and take pleasure in the entire process.

LAW 22: PRACTICE KAIZEN
[ ] Practice Kaizen. It can help me to form positive habits.

[ ] Use Kaizen for my exercising and plant-based eating goals.

THE THREE TRANSITIONAL TIERS
[ ] Apply the Greenprint laws via the three transitional tiers.

[ ] Overall, apply the Kaizen approach so you can make the desired change gradually.

[ ] In Tier 1: (the gradual shift), begin eating one plant-based meal a day for a maximum of eleven days.

[ ] In Tier 2: (the ramp up): begin eating eat two plant-based meals for eleven days.

[ ] In Tier 3: (the full on): now, go wholly plant-based. Now you are in full Vegan mode.

TIER 1: THE GRADUAL SHIFT
[ ] Tier 1 is all about eating one plant-based meal for eleven days.

[ ] The plant-based meal could be either your breakfast
, lunch or dinner

[ ] Alternatively, you can take your one-a-day plant-based meals in succession (that is, take one plant-based meal as breakfast in the first day; make it your lunch in the following day; and make it dinner the next day, and so on).

[ ] Choose only meals you find quite palatable and enjoy.

[ ] While you're on Tier 1 begin to discard any of these animal-based food products: cheese, eggs, honey, fish and shell fish, chicken, dairy products, beef, pork, lamb or all red meat.

[ ] During this eleven-day Tier 1 period, learn as much as you can about: plant-based living, the benefits of plant-based living; how to nourish your body; and the costs to you and society of the production of animal-based food products.

[ ] During this eleven-day Tier 1 period, always keep your Kaizen goals in mind. And the goals are: the consumption of one plant-based meal per day for 11 days plus the elimination of 1 or 2 animal-based food products from your diet.

TIER 2: THE RAMP UP

[ ] In Tier 2, for the next eleven days, commit yourself to eating two plant-based meals daily.

[ ] This could be breakfast and lunch or lunch and dinner. Plan whatever combination of meal that works for you.

[ ] Tier 2 is primarily about reducing your consumption of animal-based foods, while increasing your consumption of plant-based foods.

[ ] Cut out more animal-based foods from your diet.

[ ] Stay motivated. You can do this! At this time, it is important for you to always review the reasons for and benefits of a plant-based diet and the consequences of consuming animal-based products (both in terms of the impact on health, and on the environment).

[ ] If you do this constantly it will keep you motivated and you won't stray from the plant-based lifestyle progress that you are making. Once this sinks in, there's no stopping you now!

TIER 3: THE FULL-ON

[ ] In Tier 3, for the next forty-four day period, begin to eat three plant-based meals and snacks every day, in other words, you'll have to go 100% plant-based!

[ ] At this stage, remove any and all traces of animal-based food products from all of your meals.

[ ] Do not worry about animal-sourced proteins. Replace them with plant-based proteins.

[ ] Pay absolute attention to products or food information/labels and avoid foods that contain gelatin or rennet and other animal products like eggs and dairy products.

[   ] Look for and try out some good vegan restaurants. Remember that there are some continental or ethnic restaurants, Chinese, Indian, Japanese, Mediterranean, and Mexican restaurants that serve a variety of plant-based foods. Try them all! Have fun!

[   ] **HAVE FUN!** (the boldened upper case is on purpose). Have fun! Have a ball and enjoy yourself!

Made in the USA
Middletown, DE
05 July 2019